Proclaiming God's Two-Edged Sword

A Biblical Study in Confrontational Preaching

Kenneth P. Searle

Foreword by Charles E. Hackett
National Director of Home Missions
Assemblies of God

Proclaiming God's Two-Edged Sword

A Biblical Study in Confrontational Preaching

Kenneth P. Searle

ISBN 0916573-99-0

PUBLISHED BY:
BRENTWOOD CHRISTIAN PRESS
4000 BEALLWOOD AVENUE
COLUMBUS, GA 31904

Dedication

With gratefulness in my heart to God for my wife, Diane, who has blessed me more than words can express, and our three wonderful children, Jason, Amy, and Kendra, I dedicate this work to the Glory of God and the good of His Church.

Contents

Foreword

What a powerful book dealing with powerful preaching! The book is well written, easy to read and scripturally sound. This book will bring new courage and boldness to those who are called to "Preach the Word." I have not seen this subject dealt with in such a scholarly manner, and yet retain the "punch" that is missing in much of today's preaching. Dr. Searle has brought into clear focus the value and power of confrontational preaching, yet he has retained a healthy balance that will preserve the fruit of the message. This is not a book about how to rant and rave, but an excellent guide on how to address sin and bring about change that builds the church and glorifies God. Every preacher needs to read this book.

—*Charles E. Hackett*
National Director
Division of Home Missions
Assemblies of God

Acknowledgements

Books are seldom, if ever, solo efforts. This book is no exception. I spent the lonely hours researching and writing, but others helped me with proofreading and word processing.

Many thanks go to the 20 preachers who took the time to read this book in its rough form and give valuable comments. Among them, Chaplain George Rathnell went above the call of duty. Dr. Jay Adams who served as my interim faculty advisor at Westminster Theological Seminary in California gave many helpful suggestions, as did the Reverends Ken Gage and Jerrien Gunnink, and the Rev. Dr. Roger Houtsma.

Special thanks to Dr. Joe Pipa, director of Advanced Studies at Westminster Theological Seminary in California, who guided the book through its final stages.

To my father-in-law, Howard Stillwell, for his faithful exhortations to stay at the task, I am grateful.

Rich Zuris processed several drafts of this book, including the final one; with his computer expertise he accomplished wonders for which I am indebted. Thank you, Rich. Special thanks also go to Tom Wise for computer help on earlier editions.

I here wish to acknowledge the following publishers who granted me permission to quote from their published works:

Abingdon Press for Ingvar Haddal, *John Wesley: A Biography* (translated from the original Norwegian), Abingdon Press: New York & Nashville, 1961;

Anthony Douglas Publishing Co. for Mario Murillo, *No More War Games* (Chatsworth, CA, 1987);

Baker Book House for *Calvin's Commentaries* (Vol. XXI), translated by Wm. Pringle from the original Latin (Grand Rapids, Baker Book House, reprinted, 1979);

Broadman Press for A. T. Robertson, *A Grammar of the Greek New Testament in the Light of Historical Research* (Nashville: Broadman Press 1915. Renewal 1943 Ella B.

Robertson). Used by Permission, A. T. Robertson, *Word Pictures In the New Testament*, Vol. IV. The Epistles of Paul (Nashville: Broadman Press 1931). Used by Permission;

Moody Press for *Theological Wordbook of the O.T.*, R. Laird Harris, Archer L. Gleason, Waltke K. Bruce (Chicago: Moody, 1980);

Wm. B. Eerdmans Publishing Co. for Kittel, *Theological Dictionary of the N.T.*; Spurgeon, *The Soul Winner*; and White, *Expositor's Greek Testament*;

Thomas Nelson Publishers for Bruce Wilkinson and Kenneth Boa, *Talk Thru the Bible* (Nashville, Camden, N. Y.; Thomas Nelson, 1983) and Hendrickson Publishers, Peabody, MA for *The Complete Works of John Wesley*.

Many others have contributed to this effort, who are not here mentioned; they are no less appreciated.

My prayer is that this book will bring preachers back to their task of boldly proclaiming the glorious Gospel of our Lord Jesus Christ.

Introduction

D. Martyn Lloyd-Jones writes:

> ...the most urgent need in the Christian Church today is
> true preaching; and as it is the greatest and the most urgent
> need in the Church, it is obviously the greatest need of the
> world also.[1]

Preaching is an exhilarating and exacting task. It is the
means by which people come to faith in Christ for eternal life. It
is also a means by which people find direction, consolation, and
purpose.

> Real preaching from the New Testament is a desperately
> exacting task. It requires a lot of knowledge to which there is
> no easy road. But it is a tremendously rewarding task which,
> when properly done, pays rich dividends to both the congre-
> gation and the preacher himself.[2]

This book gives no panacea for easy sermon preparation.
Nor does it major on techniques, although they are included.

> The essential secret is not mastering certain techniques
> but being mastered by certain convictions. . . . Technique can
> only make us orators; if we want to be preachers, theology is
> what we need.[3]

The Biblical underpinning that supports the conviction that
preaching is confrontational is presented in this book.

It introduces and develops questions that conscientious
preachers need to ask themselves, namely, "Is my sermon appropriately confrontational?" or "Does my sermon have an
appropriate level of confrontation?" Many preachers have seldom, if ever, entertained those questions. Thus the need for this
book. When you recognize the validity of the questions, you will
find ways to adapt your preaching appropriately.

Endnotes

1. D. Martyn Lloyd-Jones, *Preaching & Preachers, (Grand* Rapids: Zondervan Publ. House, July, 1971), p. 9.

2. Morton S. Enslin, "Preaching from the New Testament: An Open Letter to Preachers" from *The Joy of Study: Papers on New Testament and Related Subjects* presented to honor FREDERICK CLIFTON GRANT, edited by Sherman E. Johnson (New York: Macmillan, 1951).

3. John R. W. Stott, *Between Two Worlds: The Art of Preaching in the Twentieth Century* (Grand Rapids: Wm. B. Eerdmans Publishing Company, 1981), p. 92.

1
What Is Confrontational Preaching

The angry mob, driven with hate, gripped sharp stones and disdainfully waited to hurl their common weapons at the impertinent preacher.

"How dare he say those things to us?" they demanded. "Who does he think he is?"

"You men who are stiffnecked and uncircumcised in heart and ears are always resisting the Holy Spirit; you are doing just as your fathers did. Which one of the prophets did your fathers not persecute? And they killed those who had previously announced the coming of the Righteous One, whose betrayers and murderers you have now become; you who received the law as ordained by angels, and yet did not keep it." These were the preacher's uncompromising words.

"We will not hear this!"

As rocks tore his skin and bludgeoned his head, Stephen, the first Christian martyr, sealed his testimony with his blood. Stephen's confrontation with the Synagogue of the Freedmen cost him his life.

Courageous confrontation characterized Stephen's proclamation. Courageous confrontation characterized much New Testament preaching, as this book will seek to show.

Toward a Definition of Confrontational Preaching

Confrontational preaching is easier to define, if you first know what it is not. Therefore, let me start with a disclaimer.

What Confrontational Preaching is Not

Confrontational Preaching is not a bludgeoning or berating of your hearers; it is not riding your favorite hobby horses, or touting your pet peeves at your listener's expense.

A preacher once filled the pulpit in Epworth, England, for

John and Charles Wesley's father, Samuel, when the famous revivalists were still boys. The congregation stopped attending the services, because the preacher—regardless of his text—would always preach on the duty to pay debts. Suzannah, John and Charles's mother, began reading Samuel's old sermons to the children Sunday afternoons to ensure that the children learned more than simply, "pay your debts." Upon hearing of Suzannah's regimen with the children, the congregants asked if they could sit in. The meetings grew so large that more towns-folk came to hear Suzannah reread Samuel's sermons than had attended Samuel's original preaching of them. Upon returning from the extended trip that occasioned such measures, Samuel wanted to test the preacher whom Suzannah said could only preach on paying one's debts.

> Wesley . . . asked: 'I suppose you can prepare a sermon upon any text I give you?'
>
> 'Yes, sir,' answered the locum (i.e.,interim supply preacher).
>
> 'Then prepare a sermon on Hebrews 11:6, "Without faith it is impossible to please God."'
>
> 'Very good.'
>
> But when the time came for the locum to deliver his sermon and the text had been read, he began thus: 'Friends, faith is a most excellent virtue, and it produces other virtues also. In particular, it makes a man pay his debts.'[1]

Confrontational preaching is not badgering hearers from every conceivable text of Scripture with the need to pay their debts—or any other favored topic. Confrontational preaching is one aspect of faithful Biblical exposition—or "true preaching," in the words of D. Lloyd-Jones—an aspect that all noted preachers of the Christian era have used, whether consciously or unconsciously.

A Dictionary Definition for "Confrontation"

The term "confrontation" is derived from two Latin words; *com-* and *frons*. *Com* means, "together," and *frons* means "forehead." These two Latin words later merged to create the French word *"Confronter,"* meaning "to confront." Our modern colloquialism, "Let's put our heads together," or "get your head together" approximate the combination of the words, though they do not capture the meaning. The meaning might be closer to the street-wise statement, "Get out of my face."

Webster gives four basic definitions for "confront." I summarize these as "facing off" factually, antagonistically, forensically, and comparatively.

Facing Factually

Webster's first definition of confront is "to stand facing; to face, to stand in front of." I apply this to our understanding of Confrontational preaching by calling this "facing factually." Simply put, when we are being faithful to the Gospel task, we are in fact conversing face to face with real people.

Another aspect of "facing factually" is facing with the facts. As we preach the Gospel there are certain facts that are very confrontational, yet must be proclaimed. For example, "Christ died for our sins" is a fact of "first importance" to the Gospel preacher (see I Cor. 15:3), yet I discovered that fact to be extremely confrontational when I mentioned it to a Jewish friend. The statement, "Christ's blood was shed for your sins and mine" met with a violent reaction. Sometimes, the mere statement of the facts to your friends, neighbors, or congregation sets up the confrontation. This is "facing factually."

Facing Antagonistically

Definition number two states, "to face boldly, defiantly, or antagonistically; to meet in hostility; to oppose."

Facing antagonistically has to do with the adversarial content of the Gospel to the world, the flesh, and the devil, not with the spirit or intention of the preacher toward his listeners. The preacher's heart, if truly Christian, yearns with the love of God for those he addresses. Yet, there are times when the truth he speaks, and the way he speaks that truth, are so scathing, it is hard to detect the preacher's love and concern for those addressed.

If the Lord Jesus had not finished his tirade against the Scribes and Pharisees with his "weeping over Jerusalem" (Matt. 23:37), some might argue that the one who showed the greatest love any man can show (cf. John 15:13), showed no love toward the Scribes and Pharisees.

> "Woe to you, scribes and Pharisees, hypocrites, because you travel about on sea and land to make one proselyte; and when he becomes one, you make him twice as much a son of hell as yourselves.
> "Woe to you, blind guides . . .
> "You fools and blind men . . . " Matt. 23:15-17—NASV

As you will see, the biblical preachers, both in the Old and New Testaments, did a great deal of this type of preaching. This is "facing antagonistically."

Facing Forensically

The third definition is, "To set face to face; to bring into the presence of, as an accused person and a witness, in court." As we preach, the Holy Spirit is carrying out this forensic arraignment process by convicting the listener of sin, righteousness, and judgment (cf. John 16:8).

The Gospel itself is forensic: it sentences man to hell and offers Christ as the only plea. Christ is not offered as a "plea bargain" (i.e., not as an opportunity to confess to a lesser crime), but Christ is offered as the One Who has paid in full the sinner's debt. Everyone, therefore, who hears the Gospel takes a seat in God's courtroom.

The Old Testament prophet Micah exemplifies this in his use of the phrase, "The Lord has a case against His people" (Micah 6:2). Because of this courtroom terminology some scholars have subtitled Micah's prophecy as "Israel's Day in Court."

In the New Testament, portions of the messages to the seven churches of Revelation read much like the charges against a defendant. For example, "But I have this against you, that you have left your first love" (Rev. 2:4, see also 2:14,20). This is "facing forensically."

Facing Comparatively

The fourth, and final definition is "to set together for comparison; to compare." Although the Gospel message opposes the world's message, the contrasts between the two messages are not always readily seen by the untrained or immature Christian (cf. Heb. 5:11-14). While some of the world's messages need to be compared to the Gospel message for seemingly slight, yet menacingly dangerous differences, much of the Gospel message stands in stark contrast to the religious and secular messages in the world.

For example, the New Testament makes frequent use of antithetical terms. Among them are, light and darkness (1 John 1:5,6; 2:10-11); good and evil (Rom. 7:21); the children of God and the children of the devil (1 John 3:10); love and hate (1 John 2:8-11); heaven and hell (Rev. 21:1-8); and life and death (Eph. 2:5). The Gospel does not find continuity with other world religions. It is diametrically opposed to them.

While the Bible speaks of antitheses, the world operates on a false sense of continuum. For example, people don't die and await judgment anymore, they simply reincarnate or do something else on the continuum. There are no absolutes, just varying shades of gray.[2]

Confrontational preaching encounters such falsehoods, by exposing them for what they are, and offering God's truth in their place. This is to "face comparatively."

Semantic Evaluation

Webster's four basic definitions of "confront," as applied above, i.e., "facing off" factually, antagonistically, forensically, and comparatively, give us a good understanding of the term *confrontation*. This fourfold understanding of confrontation is very useful in moving us toward a working definition of Confrontational Preaching.

Two Suggested Definitions for Confrontational Preaching

Two working definitions for confrontational preaching came from a survey I did to test-market the topic of this book. Brother (Pastor) Hamilton Scott of San Francisco defined Confrontational Preaching as, "The boldness to say to man, 'THUS SAITH THE LORD.'" That definition captures the face off between God and man and places the Word of God in ascendency. It also understands the need for boldness in proclamation. The second definition is from pastor and author, Ken Gage, of Marin County, California. His definition is, "Preaching that forces an individual to face up to his faults and shortcomings in the light of the Word of God." Confrontational preaching does not limit itself to shortcomings, but Pastor Gage rightly understood that the basis for Confrontational Preaching is not human opinion, but the Word of God, that there is some "facing up"—or "facing off"—to do, and that the work of confrontational preaching is conviction of sin that leads to repentance.

A Working Definition of Confrontational Preaching

Confrontational Preaching, therefore, is bold preaching. Confrontational Preaching is straight-forward speaking (e.g. Gal. 1:6-9; 3:1-5). Confrontational Preaching squarely addresses issues pertinent to the hearers (cf. Rev. 2:13-14,19-20; Rom. 16:17,18; 1 Cor. 5:1-8). Confrontational Preaching includes reproof, rebuke and exhortation (2 Tim. 4:2; e.g., Gal. 2:11-21). Confrontational Preaching recognizes that the message of Christ candidly and forcefully opposes the antichrist spirit in the world (Eph. 2:1-2). Confrontational Preaching is preaching God's authoritative Word (cf. 1 Cor. 2:1-5; 1 Thes. 2:13).

It is preaching that confronts the kingdom of darkness, in all its manifestations—not for the sake of confrontation, but for the sake of liberation. For the unsaved, salvation is offered. For the brokenhearted, healing is offered. For the captive, deliverance is offered. For the Christian, imaginations are cast down so that every thought might be brought captive to the obedience of Christ.

Having said all this, we recognize that confrontation is involved in every aspect of our proclamation. Yet there are certain times and contexts that demand a higher level of confrontation than others. These are times when sinful practices, doctrinal heresies, and ethical errors are threatening the health of the individual or the church. Therefore, our working definition of Confrontational Preaching will be, *"Preaching that directly and forcefully addresses people's moral, doctrinal, and ethical errors, with a hope to lead them to appropriate steps of faith and repentance."*

Endnotes

1.   Ingvar Haddal, *John Wesley: A Biography* (translated from the original Norwegian), Abingdon Press: New York & Nashville. Copyright The Epworth Press, 1961 (pp. 21-22)

2.   Dr. Jay E. Adams, lecturing at Westminster Theological Seminary in California, January, 1985, developed the idea of a conflict between the modern Western world-view (continuum), and the biblical world-view (antithesis), noting the need for the preacher to be aware that most people in his congregation have been raised on a world-view quite different than the one we find in the Bible. To present biblical views will inevitably bring conflict.

2
Basic Elements of New Testament Confrontation

"There are more instruments of warfare in the gospel armory than the average preacher commonly uses."[1] Stern rebuke and reproof are part of the preacher's arsenal. The primary command to rebuke and reprove in Paul's addresses to preachers is found in 2 Tim. 4:2. The context reads,

> 1 I solemnly charge you in the presence of God and of Christ Jesus, who is to judge the living and the dead, and by His appearing and His kingdom:
>
> 2 Preach the word; (*now comes the directions as to how you are to preach*) reprove, rebuke, exhort, with great patience and instruction.
>
> 3 For the time will come when they will not endure sound doctrine; but wanting to have their ears tickled, they will accumulate for themselves teachers in accordance to their own desires;
>
> 4 and will turn away their ears from the truth, and will turn aside to myths.
>
> 5 But you be sober in all things, endure hardship, do the work of an evangelist, fulfill your ministry.
>
> 6 For I am already being poured out as a drink offering, and the time of my departure has come (2 Tim. 4:1-6—NASV — italicized words in v. 2 are mine).

A Solemn Charge

This command to preach confrontationally is a solemn charge (4:1) from an aged apostle awaiting martyrdom (4:6). These are not the musings of a jovial old man telling his son in the faith to adapt to a particular epoch or people group, but rather it is the command of a seasoned Gospel General charging his Lieutenant to stay true to the faith and preach it forcefully.

Paul solemnly charges Timothy, "in the presence of God, and of Christ Jesus, who is to judge the living and the dead, and by His appearing and His kingdom . . ." Paul is stacking the deck. He is letting Timothy know that the presence of God bears witness to what he is saying. The presence of the Lord Jesus Christ bears witness. Christ's role as judge of all and His appearing and His kingdom are invoked in affirmation of what Paul is about to say. He is not saying, "Well, Timothy, if you feel comfortable preaching this way, go ahead. If not, don't bother." Paul is saying, "Timothy, I want you to do exactly as I say!"

As gospel preachers you and I need to heed Paul's charge to Timothy. We must let it motivate us to faithful proclamation. Even though motivational speeches are based primarily on temporal goals: i.e., more money, shorter work hours, longer holidays, a greater sense of fulfillment, or on reaching some personal goal; Paul's speech is based on the Glory of God. Paul's motivational speech to Timothy is not centered on, "What's in it for me?" Paul's charge is set in heaven, it proceeds from heaven, it returns to heaven. This is the course of all true ministry. As Paul said elsewhere, "For from Him and through Him and to Him are all things. To Him be the glory forever. Amen" (Rom. 11:36). True ministry proceeds "from Him" (cf. John 15:16; Eph. 4:8-11), is carried on "through Him" (cf. John 15:5), and is then offered back "to Him" (cf. 2 Cor. 5:9). Let this charge from the aged Apostle awaiting martyrdom motivate you to faithful proclamation of the truth.

Paul anticipates the times to come when such preaching will no longer be welcome: "For the time will come when they will not endure sound doctrine" (2 Tim. 4:3). The answer to such times is not to sugar-coat the truth and tickle the ears of the hearers but to "reprove, rebuke, and exhort with great patience and instruction" (v. 2).

The command to reprove, rebuke, and exhort comes from an aged apostle leaving the most important instructions to his successor. The presence of the Judge of All is invoked to bear witness to the charge. Confrontational preaching is required to counter ear-tickling heresy. Confrontational preaching is a nonnegotiable command.

A Specific Charge

The command to preach confrontationally is clear and direct: "Preach the word: *be instant* in season, out of season" (2 Tim. 4:2). The Greek military jargon of *epistethi*[2] is here variously translated "Be instant" (KJV), "Be ready" (NASV, NIV), "be urgent" (RSV), "urgently at all times" (LB), and "be at it" (Berkeley Version). The Berkeley Version may capture the sense the best with, "be at it." A. T. Robertson says the word means, *"take a stand," "stand upon it* or *up to it," "carry on," "stick to it."* (Ibid.) Fritz Rienecker enlarges upon this idea:

> to take one's stand, to stand by, to be at hand. The word was also used in a military sense; i.e., "to stay at one's post," but here it means "to be at one's task" and indicates that the Christian minister must always be on duty.

Being at one's task or post is not dependent on favorable winds. The game of life is not called on account of rain, nor is the preacher's task. "In season and out of season," as the King James puts it, refers to favorable or unfavorable times or seasons in God's dealings with mankind, or with a particular people group.

Speaking of seasons Paul uses compound words from *kairos*. *Kairos* is one of the Greek words for "time." Another is *chronos* from which we get "chronological." *Kairos* often speaks of the seasons of God's dealings, an opportune time or a time of judgment. Whether one is called to preach during one of God's *eukairoi*, favorable seasons, or one of God's *akairoi*, unfavorable seasons, the true Gospel preacher must faithfully preach God's Word (*logos*).

The directive to preach the *logos* delivers the preacher from confusion and condemnation regarding what to preach. Many emphasize the need to preach a *rhema* word. That is a word of immediate import and relevance. To preach the *logos* does not preclude God having a timely emphasis for a particular body of believers, or the church universal. It allows for that. But whether the sermon preached has obvious and immediate relevance or is the proclamation of a timeless truth, it must first and last be God's Word. The message must not originate with the preacher or be in opposition to the Biblical revelation. It must be, in every sense, God's *logos*.

As Paul puts it in 1 Thess. 2:13,

> And for this reason we also constantly thank God that when you received from us the word (*logos*) of God's message, you accepted it not as the word (*logos*) of men, but for what it really is, the word (*logos*) of God,[4] which also performs its work in you who believe (NASV).

As hinted at in the above quotation, man's word (*logos*) must never be substituted for God's Word (*logos*). Confrontational preaching, as I define it, is a proclamation of God's *logos*; that is, a *logos* that originates with God, which both proclaims and glorifies the Incarnate Word (*Logos*), the Lord Jesus Christ (cf. John 1:1; 2 Cor. 4:5; Rom. 11:36). The *logos* speaks of both the written and the Living Word, that is, the Bible and the Lord Jesus Christ. Both are in harmony: the first bears witness to the second, the second fulfills the first.

There is preaching that claims to be biblically confrontational that is not God's *logos* at all! Research for this book included a survey asking for definitions of confrontational preaching. One respondent was a pastor in San Francisco who included a transcript of a sermon he considered "biblically confrontational." He called for his denomination to sanction homosexual marriages as the first step to eventual full ordination of homosexuals. He entitled his sermon, "Dignity of Homosexual People."

> We must affirm homosexuality is a gift of God bestowed on some people. We must affirm homosexuality is a God-given part of creation. We must affirm that homosexuality is natural, right and good.[5]

This preacher considered his sermon a step toward cleansing the Temple. Although, I'm sure, he felt much like Jeremiah with his potter's vessel (Jer. 19), or Jesus with his whip (John 2:15), he was not speaking God's *logos*, but his own.

Homosexual marriage and ordination, although issues in some circles, are hardly consistent with the Word (*logos*) that the true herald is commanded to preach (cf. Rom. 1:26,27; 1 Cor. 6:9). The *logos* says of homosexuals, "God gave them over to degrading passions" (Rom. 1:26-27), and as such, they "shall not inherit the kingdom of God" (1 Cor. 6:9). To sanction their marriages in hopes of eventually ordaining some of them is to do irreparable violence to the message you claim to represent. No true *kerux* (i. e., Greek for *herald*, or *preacher*) of the kingdom of God would preach something so far afield. Yet today, churches—even large ones in influential cities—are "captained" by preachers who have substituted their word for God's.

Do not accommodate your message to the whims of your listeners or your own heart. For as the Apostle Paul proclaimed,

> For indeed Jews ask for signs, and Greeks search for wisdom; but we preach Christ crucified, to Jews a stumbling block, and to Gentiles foolishness, but to those who are the called, both Jews and Greeks, Christ the power of God and the wisdom of God (1 Cor. 1:22-24).

The preacher is a fisher of men. No true catch has come through substituting man's word for God's. Be faithful to proclaim God's Message (*logos*), and God will be faithful with the size and type of the catch.

Elements of Confrontational Preaching

Following the command to "Preach the word," Paul enumerates the methods available to the preacher: reproof, rebuke, and exhortation (2 Tim. 4:2). Paul then states the means of delivery: "with great patience and instruction." Care must be exercised, but the hearers must be reproved, rebuked, and exhorted.

Reproof

Jesus said that one task the Holy Spirit would accomplish after being sent to earth by the ascended Christ would be to "*reprove* the world of sin, and of righteousness, and of judgment" (KJV). *Elencho* is translated in the New American

Standard, "*convict* the world concerning sin, and righteousness, and judgment." "Reprove" and "convict" are strong words, as are the topics of sin, righteousness, and judgment. A simple discussion of these topics can breed confrontation, but add "reproof" or "conviction," and you are sure to have a show down. The New International Version translates *elencho* as "to prove wrong," stating that the ministry of the Spirit will be to "*prove* the world *wrong* about sin and righteousness and judgment." "To prove the world wrong" implies confrontation.

Rienecker defines *elencho*:

> To prove with demonstrative evidence, to convict, to reprove. It is to so rebuke another, with such effectual feeling of the victorious arms of the truth, as to bring one, if not always to a confession, yet at least to a conviction, of sin.[6]

What an incredible word. There is great drama here. The feeling (effectual), the posture (to rebuke another), and the outcome (to bring one to a conviction of sin) all point toward head-to-head confrontation between the truth of God as presented by the preacher and the truth of God as received by the listener.

Is this your mode of preaching? Do you set out to prove with demonstrative evidence the sinfulness of your audience to bring them to a conviction of sin, with hopes of a confession of sin leading to forgiveness and cleansing?

The use of *elencho* in 1 Cor. 14:24-25 demonstrates that the goal of reproof is repentance.

> But if an unbeliever or someone who does not understand comes in while everybody is prophesying, he will be convinced (a form of *elencho*) by all that he is a sinner and will be judged by all, and the secrets of his heart will be laid bare. So he will fall down and worship God, exclaiming, "God is really among you!" (1 Cor. 14:24-25,NIV)

Kittel makes this point very clear in his treatment of the word as used in the New Testament.

> It means "to show someone his sin and to summon him to repentance." This may be a private matter between two peo-

ple, as in Mt. 18:15; Eph. 5:11. But it may also be a congregational affair under the leader, as in the Pastorals: 1 Tm. 5:20; 2 Tm. 4:2; Tt. 1:9, 13; 2:15. It is also the work of the Holy Spirit in the world (Jn. 16:18). . . . The word does not mean only "to blame" or "to reprove," nor "to convince" in the sense of proof, nor "to reveal" or "expose," but "to set right," namely, "to point away from sin to repentance." It implies educative discipline. The noteworthy and impressive battle against sin which is part of NT Christianity is reflected in the rich use of elencho and related words.[7]

The New Testament preacher is in a "noteworthy and impressive battle against sin."[8] To win such a battle requires *reproof* (*elencho*).

"The Christian life is not like a war," writes Mario Murillo. "It, in fact, is a war!"[9] If that's true for the Christian life, it is certainly true for the ministry. Listen to the Apostle Paul exhort his fellow preacher Timothy: "Suffer hardship with me, as a good soldier of Christ Jesus" (2 Tim. 2:3—NASV). "But you, be sober in all things, endure hardship, do the work of an evangelist, fulfill your ministry. . . . I have fought the good fight" (2 Tim. 4:5,7—NASV). You have a battle to fight as a good soldier of Jesus Christ. "A shock comes when our synthetic warring collides with a 'real' Satan who knows this is not a war game!"[10]

> Preachers are soldiers in a battle for Christ, Paul told Timothy. As faithful soldiers, fighting the good fight, they are to assault the walls of thought that men rear up against the gospel and take captives for Christ. They are also shepherds. As good shepherds, they are to drive wolves away from the flock and rescue those sheep that wander into dangerous places. A good shepherd carries not only a staff, but a rod (a mace used to drive off wild animals) and a sling (remember David's?). The images of the pastor/preacher are images of the hard-working farmer in his struggle against weeds, the soldier fighting the enemy, the shepherd protecting the sheep: they are images of conflict. If a minister of the gospel is afraid to "fight the good fight," he does not "keep the faith."[11]

You are in a real battle for the souls of men, women, and children. Your major tool is the Gospel. Your methodology must include reproof. Let the following words reawaken your sense of call to preach the Gospel mightily, even when that proclamation involves reproof:

> Where are the men of steel who once shut the mouths of lions, exposed prophets of Baal, and pointed bony fingers at evil kings? Where are these champions who could preach chains off souls and ignite truth in the backslidden people of God?
>
> Rarely do we hear the hammer of preachers pounding the white-hot steel of a fervent church into weapons that can change America. All too often all we hear is the tinny voice of the cookie cutter clones of comfort.[12]

May God grant you the courage to proclaim truth even when it involves reproof. For surely, if God has called you to preach the truth, it must, at appropriate times, be accompanied by reproof.

Rebuke

Paul charged Timothy to "reprove, rebuke, and exhort" (2 Tim. 4:2). To adapt a manner of speaking from Second Peter, "And to all your reproof add rebuke" (see 2 Peter 1:5-8).

Epitimao, is the Greek word used in the New Testament for rebuke. "The strict meaning of the word is 'to mete out due measure,' but in the N.T. it is used only of censure."[13]

Censure is a harsh word. Webster defines the transitive verb form, "to blame; condemn as wrong; criticize adversely; express disapproval of."[14] This is close to the definition of *epitimao*, although the Greek word is much more redemptive in its emphasis and spirit than is censure with its major emphasis on criticism and condemnation instead of repentance. Arndt and Gingrich's definition of *epitimao* helps clarify this distinction by adding the explanatory definition, "also *speak seriously, warn* in order to prevent an action or bring one to an end."[15]

Rebuke does not demand, nor does it assume, harshness or rudeness. Quite to the contrary, harshness and rudeness are unnecessary because of the power of the truth. The statements do need to be direct; but because "truth is not only stranger than fiction it is stronger than fiction,"[16] the truth must be spoken in love. If you force yourself into a harsh mood or rude mode, you will not be able to bypass the natural, and even demonic, barriers set to ward off rebuke. Proverbs 16:21 (NASV) says, "Sweetness of speech increases persuasiveness." Your rebuke does not demand a harsh tone.

This is not to suggest that harshness, sarcasm, or even rudeness is forbidden. If you take your example from the Lord Jesus, you may make statements that will sound rude and harsh when rebuking.

> You fools and blind men. . . . You blind guides, who strain out a gnat, and swallow a camel. . . . Woe to you, scribes and Pharisees, hypocrites! For you are like white-washed tombs which on the outside appear beautiful, but inside they are full of dead men's bones and all unclean-ness. . . . You snakes! You brood of vipers! How will you escape being condemned to hell? (Matt. 23:17, 19, 24, 27, 33 — NIV)

In cases like this you must be sure of at least three things: 1) your information is correct, 2) your heart is right, and 3) your approach is the best possible approach.

Many begin with issue number three (i.e., "Is my approach the best possible one?"), and, in an *a priori* way, dismiss such direct discourse as always inappropriate or less effective than some other method. Enough has been said to expel that myth; any lingering doubts will be dispelled by a review of Stephen's example (Acts 7:51-53), Peter's example (Acts 8:20-23), Paul's example (Acts 13:9-11), as well as the example of the Lord Jesus given above. Reproof is sometimes merited.

You must, however, be sure that you have all the facts before rebuking or reproving your congregation. Many a parent has disciplined a child for some infraction only to discover later that the child was innocent. Make sure that your information is correct. To lambaste some book, some cause, or somebody without having all the facts can be embarrassing and dangerous.

Don't be afraid to rebuke, but make sure you are right. Otherwise you will be like the proverbial "firebrands, arrows, and death." A healthy reserve is good. To rejoice in rebuking a congregation would be twisted.

Make sure that your heart is right. On the heels of his scathing rebuke of the scribes and Pharisees, the Lord Jesus mourned over Jerusalem. This was evidence of his deep love for those he was warning.

> O Jerusalem, Jerusalem, who kills the prophets and stones those who are sent to her! How often I wanted to gather your children together, the way a hen gathers her chicks under her wings, and you were unwilling. (Matt. 23:37—NASV)

It's been said, "If you do not have a tear in your eye when you preach about hell you are not ready to preach about hell." The solution is not in ceasing to tell the whole truth, but in making sure that your heart is properly postured toward it! Before using rebuke, take inventory of your heart and make sure it is tender toward God and postured appropriately toward the people He wants you to address in His name.

Exhortation

Exhortation is the more positive side of confrontation. It encourages. Exhortation (*parakaleo*) means "to urge, to encourage, to exhort, to admonish."[17] It can also be translated "beseech," as in Romans 12:1. Paul urged, exhorted, encouraged, admonished, or beseeched his listeners in sermons, conversations, and letters to avoid acts of sin and perform acts of righteousness (Acts 17:34; 1 Thes. 4:1, and Rom. 12:1). In 1 Thes. 4:1, Paul urges (*parakaleo*) his readers to walk in a manner pleasing to God. In Rom. 12:1 Paul exhorts (*parakaleo*) the Romans to present their bodies to God as a living sacrifice. Paul practiced what he called Timothy to preach. Paul frequently used exhortations.

The "cognate" noun form of "exhortation" is *paraklete*. This noun is used for both the Holy Spirit (John 14:16) and the Lord Jesus (1 John 2:1-2). Modern translators render *paraklete*: comforter, counselor, advocate, and helper. Thus, to exhort is to help or assist another in a certain endeavor. For the Christian, that endeavor is to please God. To assist the believer the *kerux* (preacher) must urge, encourage, exhort, and admonish. This encouragement can come by affirming an area well done. In both 1 Thessalonians 4:1 and 4:10 (NASV), *parakaleo* is used to exhort people to "excel still more" in behavior they are already good at.

Exhortation, like reproof and rebuke, point toward a goal: Christian behavior and right response. Coaches exhort their teams, journeymen their apprentices, and preachers their congregations. Each looks for a desired result.

Exhortation is a necessary safeguard against wearing down the saints through a lopsided presentation of only reproof and rebuke. For God fully to accomplish His goals through your preaching you must reprove, rebuke *and* exhort.

The Need for Endurance and Instruction

Preaching that is confrontational, that contains elements of rebuke and reproof along with exhortation, will take "great patience" on the part of the preacher. If your message is palatable, the adulations may sustain you. But if you rattle the windows of your parishioners they may oppose you. They may resist. The need for patience (literally, "all patience") coupled with "instruction" (v. 2) will become perfectly evident.

Confrontational teaching demands change in both the preacher and the congregation. Change is often met with resistance, even when change is the right thing to do! Herein comes the need for patient instruction.

The Greek word used for patience is *makrothumia*. It is a compound word from *makro* meaning, "*long, or far away,*"[18] and *thumos*, meaning "*passion, hot anger, wrath.*"[19] Therefore, to be *makrothumia*, "long-tempered," is the opposite of being short-tempered. One New Testament Greek scholar pointed out that *makrothumia* referred to "longsuffering," or "patient endurance under injuries inflicted by others."[20] If you begin preaching confrontationally you will probably begin receiving injuries inflicted by others. Be patient under such circumstances. Refuse to become defensive. Simply, continue with the instruction.

The word *instruction* is from the Greek word *didache*. It means "teaching," or "doctrine."[21] Simply put, you need to keep instructing people in the way of the Lord: patiently, and faithfully. Your goal is not to release frustration, prove a point, or get back at them for their wickedness. Your goal should be similar, if not identical, to Paul's. Paul's goal was to ensure that his congregation was "sound in the faith" (Titus 1:13).

The faith here referred to was not saving faith, or mountain-moving faith, but doctrinal faith. The alternative to sound doctrinal faith is "paying attention to Jewish myths and commandments of men who turn away from the truth" (Titus 1:14). Paul clearly directs the preacher to use "sharp rebuke" in such cases. The rebuke, used appropriately, does not drive people away from the truth. It helps ensure their continuance in it!

As a preacher, you are called to proclaim God's word, not your own. The call to stay at your post includes "foul weather gear." You must preach in foul and fair weather alike; the gear is the Word of God. Stay properly outfitted: reprove, rebuke, and exhort.

Endnotes

1. William T. Ellis, *"Billy" Sunday: The Man and His Message* (Chicago: Moody Press, 1959), p. 76

2. According to A. T. Robertson, *Word Pictures in the Greek New Testament, ephistethi is* a second aorist (ingressive) active imperative of *ephistemi,* vol. IV, p. 629.

3. *A Linguistic Key To The Greek New Testament,* Vol. 2 (Grand Rapids: Zondervan Publishing House, 1980), p. 301.

4. Fritz Rienecker's comment on 1 Thess. 2:13 stresses the divine origin of this *logos.* His comment reads, "The phrase is to be connected with the participle and indicates the immediate source of the message delivered and received, while the emphatic *tou theou* "from God" is added to point to its real source (Milligan). The gen. "from God" is therefore a subj. gen. "preceeding from God, having God as its author," as its empathic position requires (Lightfoot; *Notes).* (Rienecker, *Linguistic Key,* Vol. 2, p. 246)

Robert L. Thomas adds to this conception of the preached word as the word of God by saying, ". . . but ultimately it was the word from God (*tou Theou).* To accentuate the word's ultimate source, Paul bluntly states that they were not accepting 'the word of men' . . . but what it 'actually' was—'the word of God.' Their appraisal of what they heard was accurate. Here is indication of Paul's consciousness of his own divinely imparted authority (cf. 1 Cor. 14:37). His preaching was not the outgrowth of personal philosophical meanderings, but was deeply rooted in a message given by God himself (cf. logos, 1:5,6,8)." Robert L. Thomas 1,2 *Thessalonians,* from *The Expositor's Bible Commentary* (Grand Rapids, Michigan:Regency Reference Library; Zondervan Publishing House), Frank E. Gaebelein, Gen. Editor, Vol. 11, p. 257.

5. The Reverend Robert Cromey, Rector. "Dignity for Homosexual People." Sermon Text at Trinity Church, San Francisco, CA. March 10, 1985.

6. Fritz Rienecker, A *Linguistic Key To The Greek New Testament,* Vol. 2, Romans-Revelation, translated and revised by Cleon L. Rogers, Jr. (Grand Rapids: Zondervan, 1980), p. 301

7. Gerhard Kittel, *Theological Dictionary of the New Testament* Vol. II, Translator and Editor Geoffrey W. Bromiley (Grand Rapids: Wm. B. Eerdmans Publishing Co.) p. 474

8. Ibid.

9. Mario Murillo, *No More War Games* (Chatsworth, CA: Anthony Douglas Publishing Co., 1987) p. 3

10. Ibid.

11. Jay Adams, *PREACHING TO THE HEART: A Heart-to-Heart Discussion with Preachers of the Word* (Phillipsburg, New Jersey: Presbyterian and Reformed Publishing Company, 1983) p. 18

12. Murillo, *War Games,* pp. 16,17

13. Newport J. D. White, *The Expositor's Greek Testament,* Vol. IV. (Grand Rapids: Wm. B. Eerdmans Publ. Co., reprinted 1970), Edited by W. Robertson Nicoll, p. 176

14. *Webster's New World Dictionary of the American Language: College Edition* (Cleveland and New York: The World Publishing Company, 1959) p. 236

15. Arndt and Gingrich, *Greek-English Lexicon, p. 303*

16. William Hendricks, "Jeremiah in Monologue" (A video presentation of Jeremiah's last days in Jerusalem delivered and recorded at a Baptist Church in Texas and on file at the Golden Gate Baptist Theological Seminary Library, Mill Valley, CA)

17. Fritz Rienecker, *A Linguistic Key to The Greek New Testament*. Translated by Cleon L. Rogers, (Grand Rapids: Zondervan.) p. 302

18. G. Abbott-Smith, *A Manual* Greek *Lexicon of the New Testament* (New York: Charles Scribner's Sons, 1936) p. 276

19. Ibid., p. 210

20. Fritz Rienecker, *A Linguistic Key to The Greek New Testament,* Vol. 2, Translated and revised by Cleon L. Rogers, Jr. (Grand Rapids: Zondervan Publishing House, 1970). A comment on Gal. 5:22, p. 171.

21. G. Abbott-Smith, op. cit., p. 114

3

How to Preach Confrontationally

During my early years as a preacher, I "naturally" preached confrontationally, but I soon stopped because I was criticized for doing so. After discovering that confrontational techniques were used by the Apostles, who preached under the anointing and inspiration of the Holy Spirit, I was liberated to return to my roots and preach as God intended.

As you read this book you may realize that you originally preached in a confrontational manner, but as well-meaning teachers, preachers, friends, or parishioners "corrected" you, you deleted certain elements from your preaching that God had "naturally" put in. Don't take out what God put in.

Use the Second Person

The Biblical preachers used a variety of pronouns in their speaking, as is common in most—if not all—spoken languages. The first and third person are often used to explain the objective truths of the Gospel. Yet when it comes to application—and at other times, as well—the second person is the pronoun of choice.

Non-Scriptural Examples

"Kenny, you mustn't say 'you' when you preach," an older Christian told me. "Say, 'we' or 'they'. You make people feel uncomfortable when you say, 'you.'"

Does this sound like good counsel? I respected the person who gave it. I was about 19 years old at the time (I began preaching at age 18). So I stopped referring to congregations as "you." Did I do right? Should I have kept calling audiences, "you"?

Let's look at my "counselor's" statement. Of the 21 words she used, six of them were "you," the very word she was instructing me **not** to use. After deleting the references to **my** use of "you," we have four uses of **you** in her directive. That's nearly 19% of the words chosen to communicate to me. Adding the references to my use of "you" mentioned in her speech, nearly 29% of the words used were the second person pronoun "you."

Why would someone believe the second person should not be exercised in pulpit speech, yet use it so freely in private speech? Because it communicates! It's direct, personal, and poignant. It adds force. And direct, personal, poignant, forceful communication can make one feel very uncomfortable. Most people simply do not want to feel uncomfortable when they come to church. But the conviction of the Holy Spirit brings with it a "godly sorrow that leads to repentance." We must, then, never delete the use of the second person simply because we don't want to make people feel uncomfortable. Deleting the second person from pulpit speech weakens its force by deleting the simplest means of direct, personal, and sometimes poignant speech.

Many godly and effective pastors and preachers who have not attended seminary may think that this point is unnecessary to mention. Nevertheless, the point is necessary. Unless there has been a major shift in the teaching of homiletics in some seminaries in recent days, there is still a wide-spread effort to discourage the use of the second person in preaching.

In a series of "Lectures on Preaching" taped in 1989 at Golden Gate Baptist Theological Seminary, in Mill Valley, California, the guest lecturer told the eager students, who devoured the otherwise very inspirational lectures, to "stop referring to your congregation as 'you.' Use the more appropriate 'we.'"

Why "we"? What makes "we" more appropriate? The first person is less direct, less confrontational, and less judgmental. Some may feel that it's more Christian. It is not. All the biblical preachers used the second person freely.

The failure to use "you" is a long standing problem, as demonstrated by The Reverend James Stalker, D.D., in *The Yale*

Lectures on Preaching, 1891. At the start of his discourse to the preachers he addresses them directly using the second person. However, he abruptly shifts to a combination of first and third person pronouns. Sadder still was the fact that his text used the second person. The natural thing to do would be to retain the biblical pronoun.

> I should like to connect what I have to say with a text of Scripture, which you may remember as a motto for this occasion. Take, then, that pastoral exhortation to a young minister in I Tim. iv. 16: "Take heed unto thyself, and to the doctrine; continue in them; for in doing this thou shalt both save thyself and them that hear thee."
>
> There are three subjects recommended in this text to one in your position—first, yourself; second, your doctrine; third, those that hear you.
>
> I. Take heed unto thyself.— Perhaps there is no profession which so thoroughly as ours tests and reveals what is in a man—the stature of his manhood, the mass and quality of his character, the poverty or richness of his mind, the coldness or warmth of his spirituality. These all come out in our work, and become known to our congregation and the community in which we labour.[1]

What did Dr. Stalker do with "you"? He has ignored "you" to speak of this other person who somehow represents you . . . or us . . . or somebody. Like so many preachers from ours and the previous century, he never made his way back to "you."

If you do not want to use the second person when you are building an outline from a text that is non-directive, fine. But if your text is built: "Point 1—Yourself . . . Point 2—Your . . . Point 3 . . . you," at least *leave it in!* Initially, you may hesitate using the second person in your outline or development. But if it is already there, do not take it out. If you do, your communication will be weakened and your text misrepresented. Preach the Word as it's written.

The following excerpt from C. H. Spurgeon's *Metropolitan Tabernacle Pulpit* demonstrates how one great pulpiteer effectively utilized the second person confrontationally.

Are **you** the victims of discontent? Young men, do **you** feel that **you** never can be contented while **you** are apprentices? Are **you** impatient in **your** present position? Believe me that, as George Herbert said of incomes in times gone by, "He that cannot live on twenty pounds a year cannot live on forty," so may I say: he who is not contented in his present position will not be contented in another though it brought him double possessions. If **you** were to accumulate property, young man, until **you** became enormously rich, yet, with that same hungry heart in **your** bosom **you** would still pine for more. When the vulture of dissatisfaction has once fixed its talons in the breast it will not cease to tear at **your** vitals. Perhaps **you** are no longer under tutors and governors, but have launched into life on **your** own account, and yet **you** are displeased with providence. **You** dreamed that if **you** were married, and had **your** little ones about **you**, and a house, all **your** own, then **you** would be satisfied: and it has come to pass, but now scarcely anything contents **you**. The meal provided to-day was not good enough for **you**, the bed **you** will lie upon to-night will not be soft enough for **you**, the weather is too hot or too cold, too dry or too damp. **You** scarcely ever meet with one of **your** fellow-men who is quite to **your** mind: he is too sharp and rough-tempered, or else he is too easy, and has "no spirit;" **your** type of a good man **you** never see: the great men are all dead and the true men fail from this generation. Some of **you** cannot be made happy, **you** are never right till everything is wrong, nor bearable until **you** have had **your** morning's growl. There is no pleasing **you**.[2] (Emphasis mine.)

To be sure, there are times to use the hortatory subjunctive, i.e., "*Let us* press on to know the Lord." The preacher does not stand above the congregation in any sense of worth or importance. He shares a common faith and pilgrimage.

The preacher also speaks for God. God is not to be lumped together with the hearers as though God also needed to come to faith and repentance. God is still looking for a mouthpiece. As Peter states, "Whoever speaks, let him speak, as it were, the utterances of God" (1 Peter 4:11—NASV). Be free to use "you."

Second Person Usage in Acts

The book of Acts contains sermons and discourses of many kinds: evangelistic sermons to both Jewish and Gentile audiences (Acts 2:14-40; 10:34-43; 13:14-48); explanations for miracles, which became platforms for proclamation (Acts 3:11-26; 4:8-12; also Acts 2:14-16); defenses before kings and governors, and before rabid crowds hoping to find grounds on which to kill the preacher (Acts 21:36-22:22; 22:30-23:10; 24:10-21; 26:1-30); personal testimonies (Acts 26; 27:21-26); personal exhortations (Acts 9:17; 27:33-34), and personal rebukes (Acts 8:20-23; 13:8-12). In all these discourses the pronoun used to address the audience is the second person "you." The first person plural "we" is not used to address audiences. In the book of Acts "You" is the pronoun of preference.

However, in some discourses the dominant pronoun is not the second person. Pronoun choice hinges on the emphasis of the specific sermon. For example, the objective reality of the Gospel demands much use of the third person "he" in describing the life, ministry, death, resurrection, and ascended glory, majesty, and power of the Lord Jesus. In other words, the kerygma calls for ample use of the third person singular (Acts 2:22-33). Another dominant pronoun in some discourses is "I." Paul, for example, uses his personal testimony to defend his life and preach the Gospel (Acts 22:3-21). He tells his story in the first person.

When the first person plural "we" is used in the sermons and discourses recorded in the book of Acts, it does not refer to the audience (the common use of "we" in preaching today), but it refers to the proclaiming body, either the apostolic community or the men on trial (Acts 4:9,20). Even in this context, the audience is referred to in the second person.

> Then Peter, filled with the Holy Spirit, said to them, "Rulers and elders of the people, if **we** are on trial today for a benefit done to a sick man, as to how this man has been made well, let it be known **to all of you**, and **to all the people of Israel,** [notice how clearly the audience is designated—no

37

ambiguous use of the first person plural here!] that by the name of Jesus Christ the Nazarene, whom you crucified, whom God raised from the dead—by this name this man stands here before you in good health. He is the STONE WHICH WAS REJECTED by you, THE BUILDERS, but WHICH BECAME THE VERY CORNER STONE (Acts 4:7-11—NASV - notes and emphasis mine).

Notice how Peter inserts the words, "by you," into the quote from Psalm 118:22! Can there be any doubt as to the preferred pronoun for preachers in the New Testament era?

"We" is used to refer to the preachers, "for **we** cannot stop speaking what **we** have seen and heard" (Acts 4:20). "You" is the pronoun used to address the audience, "Whether it is right in the sight of God to give heed **to you** rather than to God, **you** be the judge" (Acts 4:19).

Use of the Second Person in The Epistles

The Epistles are consistent in their use of "we" and "you," although there are times when "we" is used to refer to both author and reader, as does the writer of Hebrews (Heb. 12:9,10) to illustrate a point. Yet, even in this example the second person precedes the illustration and is quickly returned to.

> 7 It is for discipline that you endure; God deals with you as with sons . . .
>
> 8 But if you are without discipline . . . then you are illegitimate children and not sons.
>
> 9 Furthermore, we had earthly fathers to discipline us, and we respected them; shall we not much rather be subject . . .
>
> 10 For they disciplined us . . . that we may share . . .
>
> 13 and make straight paths for your feet . . . (Hebrews 12:7-10,13—NASV)

In most of the Epistles, the distinction is seldom blurred; the proper pronouns are consistently used. For example, Paul in Second Corinthians chapters 1, 2, and 3 uses "we" a great deal, always to refer to the Apostolic community of which he is a part. When referring to his readers he uses "you." For example,

"But I call God as witness to my soul, that to spare **you** I came no more to Corinth. Not that **we** lord it over **your** faith, but are workers with **you** for **your** joy; for in **your** faith **you** are standing firm" (2 Cor. 1:23, 24 - emphasis mine).

To increase epistolary examples would belabor the point. It is obvious that the New Testament writers and speakers addressed their audiences in the second person and themselves in the first person as is consistent with simple rules of grammar. It is not more appropriate, nor more spiritual, to do otherwise. When you preach, use the second person.

The Example of Jesus

The Lord Jesus is our ultimate example in all matters of faith and practice. He used the second person to direct his message to his hearers hearts and minds! Whether in an exhortation to the crowds and his disciples, such as the Sermon on the Mount, or in the scathing remarks addressed to his opponents, the Scribes and Pharisees (Matt. 23), the Lord Jesus used the second person to address his crowds.

In the Sermon on the Mount, for example, He used the second person to address the crowd from the end of the beatitudes (his ninth sentence) through the end of the sermon (three chapters later). There are obviously too many examples to note here.- One will suffice. Note how the Lord Jesus transitions out of the beatitudes into the remainder of His discourse:

> Blessed are you when men revile you, and persecute you, and say all kinds of evil against you falsely, on account of Me. Rejoice, and be glad, for your reward in heaven is great, for so they persecuted the prophets who were before you. You are the salt of the earth. . . . You are the light of the world. . . . Let your light shine . . . (Matt. 5:11-16)

In studying the Sermon on the Mount, the longest extant sermon by the Lord Jesus, it becomes obvious that the second person pronoun was His pronoun of choice. Shouldn't it be yours as well?

Use The Imperative

The New Testament is filled with commands. The imperative became a way of life for the New Testament preacher. Key examples in the New Testament include John the Baptist with Herod (Mark 6:17-28); Jesus with the Scribes and Pharisees (Matt. 23 and 27:1,20); Stephen with the men from the Synagogue of the Freedmen (Acts 6:8-8:1).

No one ever loved the church of Jesus Christ more than Jesus did. Yet in "The Great Commission," the Lord Jesus referred to his ministry to the disciples as one filled with commands to be obeyed. "Teaching them to observe all that *I commanded you*" (Matt. 28:20—emphasis mine). The job of the apostolic community was to make sure those commands were followed.

Paul, speaking of the "house rules" that Christians should live by, told Titus, "These things speak and exhort and reprove with all authority. Let no one disregard you" (Titus 2:15—NASV). The Greek word for *authority* is *epitages*, which is the noun meaning "command, order, injunction."[3] Moulton and Milligan, as quoted by Arndt and Gingrich, translate this phrase, "with all impressiveness."[4] The phrase, "Let no one disregard you," reinforces that Titus is to speak with full authority. This statement is in the imperative mood (a command). The verb means, "to think around someone, to despise someone, to overlook, to disregard."[5] In other words, Titus must ensure that his audience obeys his commands. He is to make sure his listener's do not despise, overlook, disregard, or think their way around his commands. A confrontational sermon filled with commands is hard to side-step. Surely, that is how Titus fulfilled Paul's directive.

In another example, the Apostle Paul wrote, "Now we command you, brethren, in the name of our Lord Jesus Christ, that you avoid every brother who leads an unruly life and not according to the tradition which you received from us. . . ." (2 Thes. 3:6) Paul is not content merely to use an imperative verb form to command his hearers to obey. He tells them that he is *commanding them* to comply. By way of application, you might command your congregation to stop gossiping, and if they don't stop, command the rest of the congregation to avoid those who persist in this sin. If that sounds harsh, take another look at 2 Thes. 3:6 above. The sin mentioned there was an *undisciplined* or *disorderly (unruly)* lifestyle! Surely gossip is as culpable as is disorderly conduct. Preach against it. Expose the sin.

You may find this difficult sledding. Many churches and Christians ignore passages that deal with church discipline. Yet church discipline is commanded in the Bible.

The most commonly ignored directives on church discipline are the instructions of the Lord Jesus in Matthew 18:15-17.

> 15 And if your brother sins, go and reprove him in private; if he listens to you, you have won your brother.
> 16 But if he does not listen to you, take one or two more with you, so that BY THE MOUTH OF TWO OR THREE WITNESSES EVERY FACT MAY BE CONFIRMED.
> 17 And if he refuses to listen to them, tell it to the church; and if he refuses to listen even to the church, let him be to you as a Gentile and a tax-gatherer (NASV).

Most people ignore this commandment simply because they don't want to be bothered. But the first command, "go" (*hupago*) is a present imperative which "often is used to express an order involving motion."[6] In other words the Lord is saying, "Get off your duff, and do it!" Overcoming inertia and getting involved is a necessary ingredient for successful discipleship. Confrontational preaching constantly reminds the congregant of that fact.

The Apostle Paul gives a similar construct for retrieving an erring church member.

> Brethren, even if a man is caught in any trespass, you who are spiritual restore such a one in a spirit of gentleness; looking to yourself, lest you too be tempted. (Gal. 6:1, NASV).

If such reconciliation proves futile, another command sheds light on the issue: "Reject a factious man after a first and second warning, knowing that such a man is perverted and is sinning, being self condemned" (Titus 3:10-11). If somebody jumps to the defense of the erring brother or sister and tries to revolt against the pastoral or church board authority that made such a "harsh" decision, another command would come into play:

> Now I urge you, brethren, keep your eye on those who cause dissensions and hindrances contrary to the teaching which you learned, and turn away from them (Rom. 16:17).

If people refused to turn away from such people an overriding command would come into play.

> Obey your leaders and submit to them for they keep watch over your souls, as those who will give an account. Let them do this with joy and not with grief, for this would be unprofitable for you (Heb. 13:17—NASV).

Commands, Not Suggestions

Do you recoil at such severities? If so, ask yourself whose word you have been preaching if the clear commands of Scripture are effrontery to you. Is such preaching an affront, or is it merely the inescapable task of every true preacher of the Gospel? This is not a question for mere academic discussion. Your application is your answer.

Not all uses of the imperative are so emotionally charged. I've used the biblical commands on avoidance and excommunication because they are so severe to our 20th century, man-centered, offend-no-one mentality. Yet they are commanded in Scripture. Rules are to be obeyed not broken. "Moses," it's been stressed, "did not deliver the ten suggestions!"

To preach biblically, you will often command your audiences to do, or abstain from doing, certain things. Make such commands without apology. In such cases you are not making suggestions, you are giving orders.

Positive Biblical Commands

The New Testament abounds in positive commands. They are still *commands.* and the Word of God commands you to command your congregation to observe all that Christ commanded his disciples to do! (Matt. 28:20) Here are some examples of positive commands from Paul's letters. "Put on a heart of compassion, kindness, humility, gentleness and patience. . . . Devote yourselves to prayer. . . . Conduct yourselves with wisdom toward outsiders, making the most of the opportunity. . . . Rejoice always; pray without ceasing; in everything give thanks; for this is God's will for you in Christ Jesus. . . .Examine everything carefully; hold fast to that which is good; abstain from every form of evil. Be filled with the Spirit" (Col. 3:12; 4:2,5; 1 Thess. 5:16-22; Eph. 5:18). Do likewise.

Use of Humor in Commands

Humor can also be used in commands. C. H. Spurgeon once commanded his people to "walk by faith with both feet.'" The Lord Jesus used humor to cause people to abandon the habit of worrying about the future, when he said, "Therefore do not worry about tomorrow, for tomorrow will worry about itself. Each day has enough trouble of its own" (Matt. 6:34—NIV). Or as one preacher put it, "If worrying will help, then call me up, and I'll come over and wring my hands with you."[8]

One very effective Bible teacher, after using humor to get an audience roaring with laughter, said, "Good. Keep laughing. That way I can punch you in the teeth without splitting your lip."[9] Humor causes defenses to come down. God's goal is obviously not to punch you in the teeth, but he does want you to obey. Humor can help people obey.

C.H. Spurgeon had much to say about the value of humor in preaching. Here is an excerpt.

> I would sooner use a little of what some very proper preachers regard as a dreadful thing, that wicked thing called humour,—I would sooner wake the congregation up that way than have it said that I droned away at them until we all went

to sleep together. Sometimes, it may be quite right to have it said of us as it was said of Rowland Hill, "What does that man mean? He actually made the people laugh while he was preaching." "Yes," was the wise answer, "but did you not see that he made them cry directly after?" That was good work, and it was well done. I sometimes tickle my oyster until he opens his shell, and then I slip the knife in. He would not have opened for my knife, but he did for something else; and that is the way to do with people. They must be made to open their eyes, and ears, and souls, somehow; and when you get them open, you must feel, "Now is my opportunity; in with the knife." There is one vulnerable spot in the hides of those rhinoceros sinners that come to hear you; but take care that, if you do get a shot through that weak spot, it shall be a thorough gospel bullet, for nothing else will accomplish the work that needs to be done. If you possess natural humor, use it. If not, cultivate it.[10]

More Drastic Measures

There are some measures beyond the imperative and the second person. They include,

Finger Pointing and Name Calling

Jeremiah was unafraid to speak the Word of The Lord to his generation. It cost him much rejection and heartache, but he remained faithful regardless the cost (Jer. 12:6; 20:7-9).

To maintain the integrity of God's message, Jeremiah pointed the finger (assumed by some of the statements: you'd have to sit on your hands not to point the finger with some of these statements), and called God's opponents by name. Listen how confrontational Jeremiah's words are on all fronts. Note the use of the second person, and predictions (in the place of commands), as well as the categorizing.

Pashur the Priest ordered Jeremiah beaten and put in stocks. Upon Jeremiah's release, the prophet exclaims:

> Pashur is not the name the Lord has called you, but rather Magomassabib. For thus says the Lord, "Behold, I am going to make you a terror to yourself and to all your friends; and

while your eyes look on, they will fall by the sword of their enemies. . . . And you, Pashur, and all who live in your house will go into captivity; and you will enter Babylon, and there you will die, and there you will be buried, you and all your friends to whom you have falsely prophesied" (Jer. 20:3,4,6).

Not only did Jeremiah name names, he changed names. Pashur was changed to Magomassabib, "Terror on every side." In the three verses noted, the second person, in various forms (you, your, yourself) is used a dozen times. Twelve uses of the second person in three sentences! With difficulty would one restrain his finger from waving in the face of his adversary as he delivered this word.

The second example is not directed to the priest, but to the King. King Zedekiah seeks a Word from the Lord regarding a battle against Babylon.

"And I myself shall war against you with an outstretched hand and a mighty arm, even in anger and wrath and great indignation . . . Then afterwards," declares the Lord, "I shall give over Zedekiah king of Judah and his servants and the people, even those who survive in this city from the pestilence, the sword, and the famine, into the hand of Nebuchadnezzar king of Babylon" (Jer. 21:5,7).

God, speaking through Jeremiah, names both the one to be judged and the one who will carry out the sentence. Jeremiah makes similar statements to the prophets Hananiah (28:15-16), Zedekiah and Ahab (29:21-23), and Shemiah (29:31-32).

Certainly, naming names and pointing fingers was fair game in the Old Testament era, but what about in the New Testament?

Categorizing

The New Testament has an interesting "parallel" to this when Paul quotes "Chloe's people" (NASV) as his source of information regarding what was going wrong at Corinth (1 Cor. 1:11). Paul also identifies different ones who categorized themselves as "of Paul," "of Apollos," "of Cephas," and "of Christ" (1 Cor. 1:12). Once Paul identified these factious groups, he attacked their theology. Through the use of sarcasm, Paul demonstrated how ludicrous were the presuppositions that established such divisive practices.

Quoting a Cretan prophet, Paul writes,

"Cretans are always liars, evil beasts, lazy gluttons." This testimony is true. For this cause reprove them severely that they may be sound in the faith (Titus 1:12-13—NASV).

This statement sounds racist. Was Paul merely speaking as a first century Jew who did not like Cretans? No. Paul attacks his Jewish brethren twice in the same section (see vv. 10 and 14), and many of the Cretans he is speaking of in this passage of Scripture were Jewish, as was he. So why did Paul sound so harsh and racist? Not only does he appear to be criticizing the Cretans, but he commands Titus to utilize *severe reproof* when addressing them (v. 13).

The reason for Paul's seemingly racist categorization is grounded in his awareness that cultures develop unique characteristics. These unique characteristics are what distinguishes one culture from another. Not every cultural attribute is godly. When you discover a cultural attribute in opposition to God's will, expose it and reprove those trapped in it, "that they may be sound in the faith" (Titus 1:13). Paul noted that while Cretans were liars, evil beasts, and lazy gluttons, the Jews tended toward substituting myths and commandments of men for the truth of God (vv. 12 and 14). The problems in your church or community may differ from those in Crete, but your response should be similar. Call them by name and raise up God's standard against them, that those who sit under the sound of your voice can be sound in the faith!

Paul uses nearly every marble in the confrontational bag to get his point across, including the "steelee." Name calling is like using your "steelee." Paul goes to the limit in 1 Corinthians 15:36, referring to his theological opponent as, "You fool."

This is dangerous ground in light of Matt. 5:22 where the Lord Jesus said anyone speaking like this would be guilty of "hell fire." The Greek word used in Matt. 5:22, however, is different than the word used in I Cor. 15:36. In Matt. 5:22 the Lord Jesus uses the word, *moros*, from which we get moron. In 1 Cor. 15:36, Paul uses *aphron. Aphron*, as used by Paul, deals with a "lack of commonsense perception of the reality of things natural and spiritual",[11] and *moron*, which Jesus warned against using, is a more direct attack on the person's intellect, heart and character.[12]

This is obviously more than semantic hair-splitting, for Paul would certainly not do something he knew the Lord would send him to Hell for. Neither would the Holy Spirit preserve the statement in Holy Writ without proper censure if Paul was wrong in making this statement. Paul is doing what Dr. Charles Swindoll has called "coming very close to the edge"[13] without jumping off. He goes to the limit of propriety (some would say beyond propriety) in building his argument. Modern preachers look woefully timid by comparison. Or is it sinfully timid by comparison?

The Lord Jesus categorized and censured certain groups. In Matthew 16:6, Jesus told his disciples to "beware of the leaven of the Pharisees and Sadducees." That is, Jesus warned his disciples to beware of a certain group of people with bad teaching and practice. He did so, not in a general way but specifically. "I'll tell you who to watch out for, those Pharisees and Sadducees!" Do you ever warn your people to beware of and watch out for the doctrines of the Jehovah's Witnesses, the Mormons or the New Age? When the Lord Jesus saw a religious group with great influence or a large following he took it upon himself to warn his disciples by naming the group and telling them what was wrong with the individuals or group named!

On another occasion the Lord Jesus chose to denounce **publicly** the activities of "the scribes and the Pharisees" (Matt. 23:1-33). This speech can hardly be called anything less than a tirade! Jesus berated these scribes and Pharisees, warning the people to "do as they say, but not as they do" because *what you see is not what you get!* (cf. 23:3) The Lord Jesus spent the next 30 verses exposing different areas of hypocrisy and introducing degrading epithets to describe these men! Jesus called them "hypocrites" seven times, "blind guides" and "blind men" twice each, and once he referred to them as "You blind Pharisee" (he used "you" often). He also called them "fools," "serpents," and "you brood of vipers." He used the second person before each reproof, either "You serpents, you brood of vipers," (v. 33), or "Woe to you, scribes and Pharisees, hypocrites!" These statements make modern political mud-slingers seem mild. Yet they were spoken by the Perfect Man, the Lord Jesus Christ! As the perfect man, He was 100% accurate.

Do not think that you must reach verbal perfection before you speak. You can make a mistake; you can also ask for forgiveness. Stop depriving your people of your protective covering as an overseer by being afraid to confront.

Factious groups and power-hungry individuals often rise up and threaten the unity and purpose of a local church. When rebuffed scripturally, they quiet down, repent, or leave. When left to themselves, they eventually prevail, even ousting the pastor. This can do irreparable damage to a local assembly. "Strike the shepherd and the sheep will be scattered." (Mk. 14:27) Your job includes guarding the flock of God from savage wolves (Acts 20:28-31) and, once the wolves are identified, warning the church regarding them as did the Apostle John in 3 John 9-12.

9 I wrote something to the church; but Diotrephes, who loves to be first among them, does not accept what we say.

10 For this reason, if I come, I will call attention to his deeds which he does, unjustly accusing us with wicked words; and not satisfied with this, neither does he himself receive the brethren, and he forbids those who desire to do so, and puts them out of the church.

11 Beloved, do not imitate what is evil, but what is good. The one who does good is of God; the one who does evil has not seen God.

12 Demetrius has received a good testimony from every one, and from the truth itself; and we also bear witness, and you know that our witness is true (NASV).

The Apostle John calls Diotrephes by name (v.9), he delineates the sins committed (vv. 9,10), makes a judgment about Diotrephes' relationship to Christ (v. 11), and states that if John visits he'll have more to point out (v.10). John then calls Demetrius by name, setting him up as an example to imitate (v. 12), in contradistinction to Diotrephes who—as alluded to in verse 11—is "the one who does evil." That's bold name calling.

An example of how you might incorporate "name calling" into your preaching is as follows:

Hebrews chapter 1 asks the question, "For to which of the angels did He (God) ever say, 'Thou art My Son, today I have begotten thee' (Heb. 1:5).

The answer is, "To no angel were those words spoken."

Yet, Jehovah's Witnesses teach that Jesus is Michael the Archangel. That is a false doctrine, and those who teach such doctrines must be avoided (cf. Gal. 1:6-9).

Warnings and Threatenings

Warnings and threatenings take the place of commands in 2 Corinthians chapters 10-13. While there is a lack of specific commands in this section, Paul's threats and warnings strongly persuade his readers to repent. For example, "and we (Paul and the true Apostolic community, not the "community we" of modern preaching) are ready to punish all disobedience, whenever your obedience is complete" (2 Cor. 10:6). The context intimates that Paul will use his considerable authority to challenge and even cast down those who are in rebellion to him or his Gospel (see 2 Cor. 10:2-5, 10-11; 12:19-21; 13:1-3).

> This is the third time I am coming to you. EVERY FACT IS TO BE CONFIRMED BY THE TESTIMONY OF TWO OR THREE WITNESSES. I have previously said when present the second time, and though now absent I say in advance to those who have sinned in the past and to all the rest as well, that if I come again, I will not spare anyone—since you are seeking for proof of the Christ who speaks in me, and who is not weak toward you, but mighty in you (2 Cor. 13:1-3—NASV).

Paul wants the people to repent, so he appeals to them with warnings.

> For I am afraid that perhaps when I come I may find you to be not what I wish and may be found by you to be not what you wish; that perhaps there may be strife, jealousy, angry tempers, disputes, slanders, gossip, arrogance, disturbances; I am afraid that when I come again my God may humiliate me before you, and I may mourn over many of those who have sinned in the past and not repented of the impurity, immorality and sensuality which they have practiced (2 Cor. 12:20,21).

> For this reason I am writing these things while absent, in order that when present I may not use severity in accordance with the authority which the Lord gave me for building up and not for tearing down (2 Cor. 13:10).

Sarcasm

Sarcasm was also used by preachers in the Bible. Sarcasm is defined as, "a taunting, sneering, cutting, or caustic remark; a gibe or jeer, generally ironical."[14] Sarcasm is from a Greek word translated, "a bitter laugh," which comes from the infinitive, "to tear flesh like dogs."[15]

"Ken, now you've gone too far! Are you trying to tell me that I have to be sarcastic to preach biblically?"

No, you do not have to preach sarcastically to preach biblically. But if you do preach using sarcasm you will not be violating biblical precedent or practice. To the contrary, you will be exercising an option that the biblical preachers themselves exercised. In other words, you do not have to preach sarcastically, but you may.

Isaiah's example:

God used sarcasm in the Old Testament to combat the practice of worshiping idols.

> 14 . . . He plants a fir, and the rain makes it grow.

> 15 Then it becomes something for a man to burn, so he takes one of them and warms himself; he also makes a fire to bake bread. He also makes a god and worships it; he makes it a graven image, and falls down before it. 16 Half of it he

burns in the fire; over the half he eats meat as he roasts a roast, and is satisfied. He also warms himself and says, "Ah, I am warm, I have seen the fire."

17 But the rest of it he makes into a god, his graven image. He falls down before it and worships; he also prays to it and says, "Deliver me, for thou art my god" (Isaiah 44:14-17, NASV).

Most of us snicker at the stupidity outlined above. Who in his right mind would worship the same piece of wood he used to roast his dinner over? No one. That's the point. Deceived people are not in their right minds. Their thinking is deviant. Revealing the absurdity of an aberrant position is sometimes better accomplished through the use of sarcasm than through the use of pure reason.

Paul's example:

"For you, being so wise, bear with the foolish gladly. For you bear with anyone if he enslaves you, if he devours you, if he takes advantage of you, if he exalts himself, if he hits you in the face. To my shame I must say that we have been weak by comparison" (2 Cor. 11:19-21—NASV).

"Become sober-minded as you ought, and stop sinning; for some have no knowledge of God. I speak this to your shame. But some one will say, 'How are the dead raised? And with what kind of body do they come?' You fool! That which you sow does not come to life unless it dies" (1 Cor. 15:34-36—NASV).

Stephen's example:

"Which one of the prophets did your fathers not persecute?" (Acts 7:53—NASV)

Peter's example:

"Give heed to my words. For these men are not drunk, as you suppose, for it is only the third hour of the day" (Acts 2:15—NASV). This, admittedly, is a very mild form of sarcasm and could be seen as humor.

John the Baptist's example:

John said to the crowds coming out to be baptized by him, "You brood of vipers! Who warned you to flee from the coming wrath? Produce fruit in keeping with repentance. And do not begin to say to yourselves, 'We have Abraham as our father: For I tell you that out of these stones God can raise up children for Abraham'" (Luke 3:7-8—NIV).

The Lord Jesus' example:

The obvious examples found in Matthew 23 will not be recorded here except to remind the reader of their existence. Jesus used sarcasm not only in discourse to the multitudes, as recorded in Matthew 23, but also in dealing with those in opposition to his doctrine, ministry, or life-style (Matt. 11 and 12 have several examples of this).

To the question of his opponents, "Is it lawful to heal on the Sabbath?" Jesus answered,

> "What man shall there be among you, who shall have one sheep, and if it falls into a pit on the Sabbath, will he not take hold of it, and lift it out? Of how much more value then is a man than a sheep! So then, it is lawful to do good on the Sabbath" (Matt. 12:10-12—NASV).

To those who said Jesus cast out demons by "Beelzebul the ruler of the demons," Jesus countered, "If I by Beelzebul cast out demons, by whom do your sons cast them out?" (Matt. 12:24-27)

Other New Testament examples:

James 3:19, "Thou believest that there is one God; thou doest well: The devils also believe, and tremble" (KJV). See also James 3:15-16.

Hebrews 6:1 and 3, "Let us press on to maturity. . . . And this we shall do, if God permits" (as though God would seek to oppose us from reaching maturity). Obvious sarcasm is used here from a writer who has already rebuked his readers for being immature: "by this time you ought to be teachers" (Heb. 5:12).

1 John 4:20, "If some one says, 'I love God,' and hates his brother, he is a liar; for the one who does not love his brother whom he has seen, cannot love God whom he has not seen."

Sarcasm is used frequently in the New Testament. It appears in a variety of contexts including sermons, discussions with opponents, and letters to churches.

Boldness, A Common Thread

Paul said, "I did not *shrink* from declaring to you anything that was profitable" (Acts 20:20), and again, "I did not *shrink* from declaring to you the whole purpose of God" (Acts 20:27). The word for "shrink" is *hupostello*, meaning, "to draw back in fear, to shrink from. The opposite of 'to speak boldly'."[16] New Testament preaching was bold preaching! (Acts 4:13,31; 14:3) The Star Trek generation may "boldly go where no man has gone before," but your task is to "speak boldly like those saints who **have** gone before!"

> What is boldness? The Greek word, *parresia*, means freedom in speaking, openness, willingness to be frank; it is plain speech that is unencumbered by fear. A bold preacher is one who has no fear of speaking the truth—even when it hurts. Many ministries are hampered today simply because of the fear of men. "Will Mrs. Jones take offense if I preach this?" "What will happen if I teach this to the congregation?" and similar thoughts go through the minds of far too many preachers, when what they ought to be asking themselves is, "What will God think of me if I don't teach His truth?"[17]

To take this a step further, "What would God think of me for not preaching His truth in the same manner employed by the Bible preachers?"

Guard yourself from the tendency to dismiss all this evidence as mere drivel. Any keenly organized hermeneutic that relegates Biblical examples to mere cultural captivity will ultimately force every man to do what is right in his own eyes. Do not prevent Old Testament examples from having an impact on you because you are under a New Covenant. Do not dismiss New Testament examples because you are in the Church Age rather than the Apostolic one. Let the Scriptures speak! "For **whatever** was written in earlier times was written for our instruction" (Rom. 15:4). "All Scripture is inspired by God and profitable for teaching" (2 Tim. 3:16). Let the Spirit take the Word and apply it to your preaching and teaching ministry. God is looking for fearless men who will preach His Word with power of delivery. He wants men and women, like those in the early church, who are unafraid of the consequences (Acts 4:29-30).

This fearlessness is not a work of the flesh, i.e., not a work of man. Boldness is as surely a work of the Spirit of God as is salvation. As Jay Adams writes, "The early church prayed for boldness, and the Spirit produced this boldness within them (Acts 4:29-31)."[18] Adams continues, "That is the same way that preachers must acquire boldness today."[19]

Do not try to preach confrontationally on your own. That is, if you want to preach with the same boldness as did the early church, ask for the boldness the Holy Spirit gives.

> The power of preaching is found in the Spirit working with the Word of God, and through the Word of God. God promises that His word will not return to Him void. Its power is located not in the eloquence or erudition of the preacher but in the power of the Spirit. Preaching is a tool in the hands of the Spirit of God. The Holy Spirit is a supernatural being, the Third Person of the Trinity. His presence in preaching is what makes it a supernatural event.[20]

Ask for, and receive the power of The Holy Spirit for your preaching (Lk. 11:9-13; Mk. 11:23,24). The power of the Spirit will add conviction to your preaching. The Spirit will also give you boldness.

Many preachers fear the consequences of preaching boldly. Don't. Jay Adams tells you why you need never fear preaching boldly.

> When did you ask God to make you a bold preacher? When did you ask for "all the boldness needed to speak?" Are you afraid to ask; do you fear the consequences of asking? After all, God might hear and answer your prayer! Then where would you be? Right, getting yourself into a lot of trouble, like Paul and Peter and Stephen! That would never do, would it? But, notice the interesting dilemma that I have just sketched: you are afraid to pray for boldness because you might get it, and you fear what would happen as a consequence. But don't you see the fallacy in that sort of

reasoning? You would not fear any longer if you did become bold; as a matter of fact, you fear such consequences only because you now fear consequences. It will all change when the Lord answers your prayer.[21]

Ask the Lord for boldness. Believe God to give it. Then, preach with the confrontational authority that only the Spirit can produce.

Personal Testimony and Affirmation of Love

When you begin to preach confrontationally your congregation may experience initial shock. You can ease the load by sharing your own struggle with that kind of preaching. It's best to let the confrontation do its perfect work first, however. Listen to Paul's comments on his letter that caused the Corinthians pain.

> For though I caused you sorrow by my letter, I do not regret it; though I did regret it—for I see that that letter caused you sorrow, though only for a while—I now rejoice, not that you were made sorrowful, but that you were made sorrowful to the point of repentance; for you were made sorrowful according to the will of God, in order that you might not suffer loss in anything through us. For the sorrow that is according to the will of God produces a repentance without regret, leading to salvation; but the sorrow of the world produces death (2 Cor. 7:8-10, NASV).

Confrontational preaching will sometimes cause sorrow for you and your congregation. But it is a sorrow according to the will of God. You do not have to make apology for that sorrow but you can openly discuss it. Although you must not soft-peddle your wares, you can soften the shock by articulating what may no longer seem apparent; I.e., the fact that you love your congregation and that is the reason for the "sorrow producing" sermon.

The Apostle Paul was very careful to communicate his love to those he served. In Thessalonica, the church was experiencing persecution. Paul feared that the "Tempter" may have caused these suffering saints to lose hope in God, or to believe the lie that Paul did not love them. Paul reminds them of his behavior toward them,

7 But we proved to be gentle among you, as a nursing mother tenderly cares for her own children.

8 Having thus a fond affection for you, we were well-pleased to impart to you not only the gospel of God but also our own lives, because you had become very dear to us
(1 Thess. 2:7,8—NASV).

People seldom hear that they are loved. You heard the one about the woman who, after 40 years of marriage, wanted her husband to tell her he loved her. When she brought it up, he growled, "Marge, on the day we were married I told you I loved you. When I change my mind, I'll let you know!"

People in your congregation need to hear that they are loved, even by their pastor. After teaching on how much God loves us in Christ, one of my Bible College students (who was not doing particularly well in my class) asked, "But do you?"

He was serious. He needed affirmation. I assured him I loved him; that my love was not based on how well, or how poorly, he was doing in my class. He said, "Sometimes, we just need to know you love us."

Remember, Satan is the accuser of the brethren (Rev. 12:10). If you add a substantial dose of confrontation to your proclamation, Satan will work overtime to convince your congregation that you do not care for them personally. The truth is, you are confronting them because you care. God disciplines those he loves (cf. Heb. 12:6; Rev. 3:19), and sometimes God's discipline comes through the preached word (cf. 2 Cor. 10:3-6, 8-11; 13:10).

Preach the Word, reprove, rebuke and exhort. And with all your rebuke, reproof, and exhortation make sure your congregation knows you love them (cf. Eph. 4:15).

Remember also that this kind of preaching cost the lives of some of the early preachers. Don't worry about being popular. Although you probably won't be stoned to death, you may spend some time in the unemployment line. Don't take it personally; the student is not above the teacher, nor is the slave above his master. If they said Jesus was demonized, how should they treat you (cf. Luke 6:26)? As for your part, preach the Word, and leave the results to God.

Endnotes

1. The Reverend James Stalker, D.D, *The Preacher and His Models* (Hooder and Stoughton; New York: George H. Doran Company, 1891), p. 267.

2. Charles Haddon Spurgeon, "The Overflowing Cup," from *The Metropolitan Tabernacle Pulpit* (Pasadena, Texas: Pilgrim Publications, 1971), Vol. XXI, 1875, pp. 147-148.

3. Arndt and Gingrich, *Greek-English Lexicon, p.* 302

4. Ibid.

5. Rienecker, *Linguistic Key,* Vol. 2, p. 309

6. Fritz Rienecker, *Linguistic Key To The Greek New Testament* (Grand Rapids: Zondervan, 1980) edited by Cleon Rogers, p. 54

7. C. H. Spurgeon, "The Overflowing Cup," in *The Metropolitan Tabernacle Pulpit,* Vol. XXI, p. 149.

8. Pastor Stanford A. Warner, Novato, CA, 1987.

9. Bob Mumford, speaking at a Men's Seminar, Shiloh Christian Center, Oakland, CA, c. 1987

10. Charles Haddon Spurgeon, "Sermons Likely to Win Souls," from *The Soul Winner* (Grand Rapids; Wm. B. Eerdmans Publ. Co., 1963), pp. 94-95.

11. Vines, *Expository Dictionary,* p. 113

12. Compare Arndt and Gingrich, *Greek-English Lexicon,* "The mng. of *more* Mt. 5:22 is disputed. Most scholars take it, as the ancient Syrian versions did, to mean you *fool . . .* Somet. also w.

the connotation of an obstinate, godless person (like nabal—in Heb. Nun, Beth, Lameth)" (A. and G., p. 533b and c). And Vine states "MOROS . . . primarily denotes dull, sluggish . . . hence, stupid, foolish . . . scorns his heart and character, hence the Lord's more severe condemnation" *(Vine's Expository Dictionary* p. 114).

13. Chuck Swindoll used this phrase to describe his own preaching, in a seminar the writer attended entitled, "Taking the Ho-Hum Out of Your Preaching." This seminar was at the Congress on Biblical Exposition, in Anaheim, CA, c. 1985.

14. Webster's New Twentieth Century Dictionary of The English Language: Unabridged (second edition), (United States: William Collins+World Publishing Co., Inc., 1977) p. 1608

15. Ibid.

16. Fritz Rienecker, *A Linguistic Key to The Greek New Testament* Vol. 1, Translated by Cleon L. Rogers, Jr. (Zondervan Publishing House: Grand Rapids, Michigan) p. 318

17. Jay E. Adams, *Preaching to the Heart* (Presbyterian and Reformed Publishing Company: Phillipsburg, New Jersey, 1983) pp. 16-17

18. Jay E. Adams, *Preaching To The Heart* (Phillipsburg, New Jersey: Presbyterian and Reformed Publishing Company, 1983) p. 20

19. Ibid.

20. R.C. Sproul, "What's Going On Here?", *Table Talk,* Issue entitled "The Power of Preaching" (Published by Walk Thru the Bible Ministries, Inc. under license granted by Ligonier Ministries, Inc., March 1989) p. 5

21. Jay E. Adams, *Preaching to the Heart,* (Phillipsburg, New Jersey: Presbyterian and Reformed Publ. Co., 1983), pp. 20, 21

4
Occasions for Confrontation

Introduction

Certain contexts demand confrontation. The Apostle Paul warned Titus that false teachers could "overturn whole households" (Titus 1:11). John Calvin noted that if there was danger of even upsetting one individual's faith, "The pastor should immediately gird himself for the combat; how much less tolerable is it to see whole houses overturned?"[1]

Many households have been overturned by false doctrines and practices simply because the preacher, who had access to those families, shrank from his responsibility to reprove, rebuke and exhort.

Paul refused to make that mistake. "I am innocent of the blood of all men. For I did not shrink from declaring to you the whole purpose of God" (Acts 20:26-27—NASV). To declare the whole purpose of God it is sometimes necessary to use confrontational techniques.

This chapter catalogs instances where confrontation is mandated. It then analyzes select instances as examples for instruction.

When Confrontation is Mandated

Times that demand confrontation include the following: when immaturity continues in a fellowship beyond natural, or reasonable, limits (Hebrews 5:11-12 and 1 Cor. 3:1-3); when your personal integrity and/or authority are in question (2 Cor. 10-13, Titus 2:15, and 1 Tim. 4:12); when a false gospel is being preached, or accepted, as true (Gal. 1:6-9 and 2 Cor. 11:1-4); when addressing people who are ruled by their appetites (Titus 1:12-14); when addressing the factious, i.e., those threatening the unity of the body (1 Cor. 1:10-15, 3:5-4:6; Gal. 2:11-14; Titus 3:10-11; James 4:11-12; 5:9); when saints are living presumptuously (James 3:13-16); when saints are becoming arrogant (1 Cor. 4:6-21; James 4:1-17); when saints are lapsing into the works of the flesh (1 Cor. 5:1-13; 6:9-20); when cardinal Christian doctrines are being denied (such as the resurrection of the dead—1 Cor. 15, see especially vv. 34-36, and salvation by faith apart from the law, Gal. 2:21-3:22; 4:16; 5:4,7-12); when addressing those opposing the spread of the Gospel, or those seeking to pervert the true faith (Acts 8:18-25; 13:9-12); or when false apostles, prophets, evangelists, pastors, or teachers ("wolves") threaten the sheep (Acts 20:28-30; 2 Peter 2; 2 John 7-11; 3 John 9-11).

Analysis of Specific Biblical Occasions for Confrontation

It is apparent from the above list that many issues demand a confrontational approach. You may presently be facing such an issue. Perhaps yours will be one of the issues we explore in depth in this chapter. Even if it is not you will find practical help through analyzing the ways the Biblical writers handled such potential problems.

When a Cardinal Doctrine Is Being Questioned or Denied

A key doctrine of the Christian faith is the bodily resurrection of The Lord Jesus Christ. The correlate of the Lord's resurrection is the resurrection of all believers (cf. 1 Cor. 15:20-23). In the first century a group of "believers" in Corinth challenged this correlate resurrection. Paul was quick to defend the truth and turn the attack on the opponents of sound doctrine.

In mounting his offensive, the Apostle Paul used several confrontational methods. In order to convince his listeners that the resurrection was a non-negotiable Christian doctrine, Paul used the imperative, sarcasm, the second person and reproof.

The Use of The Imperative

"Do not be deceived: 'Bad company corrupts good morals.' Become sober-minded as you ought, and stop sinning" (1 Cor. 15:33-34).

Here Paul lists three commands in two verses. The first is

60

negative, "Be not deceived." This deals with issues of the mind and spirit. The second is stated positively, "Become sober-minded." This command also deals with the thought life. The third command is quite broad; it encompasses both thought and behavior: i.e., "stop sinning."

These three examples reveal that commands can deal with various issues, or realms. The first two commands addressed inappropriate thoughts. The third command covered both thoughts and behavior.

Many preachers recognize the need to issue commands in the area of behavior. "Do not get drunk with wine" (Eph. 5:18). "Children, obey your parents" (Eph. 6:1). However, most, if not all, spiritual problems that would call forth the imperative originate in the mind. Gospel ministry involves "destroying *speculations* and every lofty thing raised up against the knowledge of God, and taking every *thought* captive to the obedience of Christ" (2 Cor. 10:5, NASV–italics mine). When you use commands, don't limit them to behavior. Deal with sinful thoughts, as well.

Paul addressed both areas in Romans 12:1, 2.

> I urge you . . . to present your bodies a living and holy sacrifice, acceptable to God, which is your spiritual service of worship . . . And do not be conformed to this world, but be transformed by the renewing of your mind . . . (Rom. 12:2)

The presentation of your body to God is maintained by the continual renewing of your mind. That is, both your thoughts and your deeds constitute your obedience. As Isaiah put it, "Let the wicked forsake his *way*, and the unrighteous man his *thoughts*" (Is. 55:7–italics mine). When you issue commands, make sure you cover both arenas. "'For my *thoughts* are not your *thoughts*, neither are your *ways* my *ways*,' sayeth the Lord" (Is. 55:8–italics mine).

When you combat heresy you will deal with issues of the mind. Exercise your liberty; tell people how to think, as well as how to act.

The Use of Sarcasm

Paul defended the veracity of the doctrine of Christ's resurrection by using sarcasm.

> 35 But some one will say, "How are the dead raised? And with what kind of body do they come?"
> 36 You fool! That which you sow does not come to life unless it dies . . .   (1 Cor. 15:35-36)

Paul also protested,

> "If from human motives I fought with wild beasts at Ephesus, what does it profit me? If the dead are not raised, LET US EAT AND DRINK, FOR TOMORROW WE DIE"
>   (1 Cor. 15:32).

In the first instance Paul is quite blunt. Paul calls his opponents fools, and reminds them that the seed you see is not the seed you get once you plant it. The seed "dies"; i.e., it goes through a transformation. So with the body.

In the second issue, Paul is a bit more subtle, though not much. He states the logical outcome of a "no-resurrection theology." That is, if there is no resurrection, there is no judgment. If there is no judgment, then what's the point in living righteously. If there is no judgment, we might as well "Eat, drink and be merry, for tomorrow we die." Anyone who knew Paul, as the Corinthians did, knew how high were his moral and ethical standards. Using sarcasm brought the ludicrous posture of a no resurrection theology into proper focus.

Don't hesitate to use sarcasm when it can effectively expose the error of a dangerous heresy.

The Use of The Second Person

Surprisingly, Paul does not make copious use of the second person in defending the doctrine of the resurrection. Rather, he develops the true doctrine objectively. When he uses the second person it is to draw attention to the heresy (1 Cor. 15:12) and to make application (1 Cor. 15:14,17,58).

The first usage of "you" in 1 Cor 15:12-58 is,

> Now if Christ is preached, that He has been raised from the dead, how do *some among you say* that there is no resurrection of the dead (v. 12 - italics mine)?

Paul wants his audience to know he is not addressing "paper tigers." Paul addressed real people who held to real heresies. You do to. Letting the church know there are heresies among them can be a way to safeguard the flock.

As noted above, Paul also used the second person to make application. The first two instances of application are in a negative construction: "If Christ has not been raised, then our preaching is vain, *your* faith also is vain" (1 Cor. 15:14). And, ". . . If Christ has not been raised, *your* faith is worthless; *you* are still in *your* sins" (1 Cor. 15:17–italics mine).

This is poignant application. "Your faith is vain (15:14). Your faith is worthless (15:17). You are still in your sins" (15:17). Can you imagine the uproar you might encounter if you started using that kind of confrontation?

The final use of "you" in 1 Cor. 15 is in a positive construction. It is also one of the most gripping imperatives in Scripture.

> Therefore, (i.e., in light of this resurrection hope), my beloved brethren, be steadfast, immovable, always abounding in the work of the Lord, knowing that your toil is not in vain in the Lord (1 Cor. 15:58—NASV).

Don't be afraid to expose and rebuke error; the outcome may prove to be as inspiring as Paul's conclusion to this great treatise on the veracity of the resurrection.

Application is the most common way to use the second person. If you shy away from its use, application is a good place to start.

Reproof

As discussed in Chapter 2 *reprove* means to convict, prove wrong, or to prove with demonstrative evidence. Paul amasses great evidence as he combats the anti-resurrection heresy that was prevalent at Corinth.

Details matter. Be specific. Argue your point from many different angles. Paul argued from nature (vv. 36-41), from logic (vv. 12-17), from theology (vv. 20-28), from reason (vv. 29-34), and from prophetic proclamation (vv. 50-58). Vary your content. Give sufficient data to prove your point with demonstrative evidence.

Don't let false doctrine prevail. God has given you the tools to keep people sound in the faith.

When Authority Is in Question

Another situation that requires confrontational preaching is when the preacher's authority or personal integrity is in question. This is often difficult for preachers to do without feeling self-serving. You are willing to defend the faith, but not your own reputation. This is a grave mistake. Paul recognized that if his credibility could be damaged, his Gospel could be ignored. Therefore, the Apostle Paul defended his reputation with the same vehemence as he defended his Gospel! His denunciations on those who attacked his character carried every bit as much force as did his defense of the Gospel.

This type of intense polemic may seem far removed from your personal pastoral experience. That may not always be the case. In one church I pastored in California, a man in our congregation with a Doctor's Degree in Science, claimed he'd had a vision from God that revealed that all reality was made up of 5 dimensions. He wrote a 360 page book on the subject and began teaching it to people every chance he got. The problem with his doctrine was that it was false. The problem with his approach was that it was insidious. The problem with his influence was that it was growing.

His doctrines were not innocuous. Here's a sample: Satan was part of his "Trinity." Actually, he rejected the term "Trinity", because Trinity is three-dimensional, not five-dimensional. But when asked to humor me because "Trinity" was the traditional Christian position on the Godhead, he revealed that the second person of his Trinity was two-dimensional, made up of the physical dimension and the spiritual dimension: Christ reigns over the spiritual, and Satan over the physical. That's only one example of his doctrinal aberrations.

He claimed that he seldom taught these doctrines to anybody in the congregation. He claimed when church people were over at his house for "counseling" he only taught directly from the Bible. When we finally had to excommunicate him for his refusal to stop teaching his weird doctrines and drawing disciples away after himself (cf. Acts 20:28-30; Matt. 7:15) we asked the crowd gathered, "How many of you has Mr. 'H' tried to teach these false doctrines to?" Of the approximately 300 gathered over one half raised their hands. His inner circle (i.e., his three primary disciples) included the local president of The Full Gospel Businessmen's Association, a young YWAM, DTS graduate who had recently returned from a mission trip overseas, and a Bible study leader in our church who had previously graduated from a good Bible College in Southern California. When I said his concept of the Trinity was blasphemous one of these men asked, "What's wrong with that?"

Paul warned,

1 But the Spirit explicitly says that in later times some will fall away from the faith, paying attention to deceitful spirits and doctrines of demons,

2 by means of the hypocrisy of liars seared in their own conscience as with a branding iron (1 Tim. 4:1,2, NASV).

I am happy to report that all three of those men were eventually restored to right doctrine, and right relationship to the body of Christ. But it was not without a fight.

We submitted his work to the late Dr. Walter Martin for critique. They (the inner circle, and Mr. "H") agreed to live by Dr. Martin's conclusions. The conclusions were consistent with our own. Mr. "H" refused to comply. He then wrote a letter denouncing me and the researcher for Dr. Martin who did the critique. Our heretic claimed, among other things, that I and Dr. Martin's researcher were simply unwilling to let the Scriptures speak. He mailed this letter to everyone on our church mailing list. Many people were hurt and confused, some sided with Mr.

"H" and eventually left the church. The vast majority, and the church at large, were protected from what might have been the beginning of another American cult.

In cases like this, defending yourself is not self-serving. As the Apostle Paul put it,

> All this time you have been thinking that we are defending ourselves to you. Actually, it is in the sight of God that we have been speaking in Christ; and all for your upbuilding, beloved (2 Cor. 12:19—NASV).

Second Corinthians is an excellent source of wisdom for those faced with the responsibility of defending themselves, as well as the Gospel they proclaim. Paul uses a full array of confrontational techniques to defend his character, authority, and ministry. Specific examples include 2 Cor. 10:1 and 11:4-5:

> Now I Paul myself urge you by the meekness and gentleness of Christ—I who am meek when face to face with you, but bold toward you when absent! (2 Cor. 10:1)

> For if one comes and preaches another Jesus whom we have not preached, or you receive a different spirit which you have not received, or a different gospel which you have not accepted, you bear this beautifully. For I consider myself not in the least inferior to the most eminent apostles (2 Cor. 11:4, 5).

In the above passages Paul uses several confrontational techniques, including sarcasm, categorizing, and reproof. He categorizes people directly and by innuendo and allusion. He proves his opponents wrong by demonstrative evidence (reproof). His words are filled with sarcasm.

Categorizing

Paul categorizes a group of "super-apostles" (11:5) whom he refers to as the infamous "some" (10:2,12). I.e., **"Some,** who regard us as if we walked according to the flesh," and **"Some** of those who commend themselves" (10:2 and 12 - emphasis mine). After Paul has identified the presence of a factious group, he then demonstrates how spurious are their claims and begins calling them some vary rough names.

Name Calling

Paul refers to these opponents as "false apostles," and "deceitful workers" (11:13). That's a severe case of name calling. He goes on to speak of their associations as being truly diabolical.

> 13 . . . disguising themselves as apostles of Christ.
> 14 And no wonder, for even Satan disguises himself as an angel of light.
> 15 Therefore it is not surprising if his servants also disguise themselves as servants of righteousness . . . (2 Cor. 11:13-15)

Sarcasm

This section is replete with sarcasm. Paul had labored to start this church and had spent 1-1/2 years as its Senior Pastor (Acts 18:1-11). A group of Pseudo-Apostles (11:5,13) had crept in and were trying to discredit Paul and his ministry. His sarcasm is clear and plenteous. Among the examples the following stand out.

> 19 For you, being so wise, bear with the foolish gladly.
> 20 For you bear with anyone if he enslaves you, if he devours you, if he takes advantage of you, if he exalts himself, if he hits you in the face.
> 21 To my shame I must say that we have been weak by comparison . . . (2 Cor. 11:1-21—NASV)

And,

> 13 For in what respect were you treated as inferior to the rest of the churches, except that I myself did not become a burden to you? Forgive me this wrong! . . .
> 16 But be that as it may, I did not burden you myself; nevertheless, crafty fellow that I am, I took you in by deceit (2 Cor. 12:13,14—NASV).

The Apostle, having paid the price to establish this church, was not willing to have evil spoken of him. He knew if he could be discredited his Gospel could be ignored, or a false gospel could be substituted for it. Therefore, Paul willingly used sarcasm to point out the absurdity of his opponent's claims, and to reaffirm his authority in the Gospel.

Although this Biblical example is not a mandate it is a permission slip. That is, you *can* use sarcasm against opponents. The Bible writers used sarcasm under the inspiration of the Holy Spirit. The same Spirit that spoke through them wants to speak through you. Don't make unnecessary limitations on how freely He can speak through you.

Reproof

As noted earlier reproof includes proving someone wrong with demonstrative evidence. Paul is so committed to demonstrating that his opponents are wrong that he takes what has become four chapters of Holy Writ to do it. 2 Corinthians 10-13 catalog statements Paul's opponents have made and his defenses based on those statements.

Take note of chapters 10 through 13 of 2 Corinthians. In Paul's personal defense he tells of his love for the Corinthians (11:7,8,11,29; 12:15), of his labors and his sufferings in the Gospel ministry (11:23-33), of his revelations of, and relationship with, God (12:1-10), of his desires for the Corinthians (10:6;11:2), of the weapons of his warfare (10:3-6), and of the purpose for his authority in Christ (10:8; 13:10). He makes sure the Corinthians know that Paul is the same by letter as he is in person, but he does not want to use his authority to tear them down but build them up. (Look how Paul keeps this thread going throughout these four chapters: 10:1,6-7,8-11; 11:6; 13:1-3,10.) He also denigrates his opponents authority to speak, stating their boasts are empty ones when compared to his own (11:13-15; 12:11-12).

Warnings and Threatenings

Paul ends this section with a warning that if repentance does not precede his return "heads will roll."

> 1 This is the third time I am coming to you. EVERY FACT IS TO BE CONFIRMED BY THE TESTIMONY OF TWO OR THREE WITNESSES.
> 2 I have previously said when present the second time, and though now absent I say in advance to those who have sinned in the past and to all the rest as well, that if I come again, I will not spare anyone—

3 since you are seeking for proof of the Christ who speaks in me, and who is not weak toward you but mighty in you. . . .

10 For this reason I am writing these things while absent, in order that when present I may not use severity in accordance with the authority which the Lord gave me for building up and not for tearing down. (2 Cor. 13:1-3, 10)

Paul had real authority. You and I do also. Church discipline has been given to the church. Matthew 18:15-20 testifies to the fact that you and I have the power to discipline members of the church. Warnings and threatenings are at times the order of the day.

Conclusion

There are times when you are faced with a confrontational issue. Do not shy away from it. In the opening paragraphs of this chapter I list over a dozen categories of behavior that call forth a confrontational approach to preaching. You may be faced with one or more such challenges. Knowledge of how Paul handled his crises, a commitment to defend the Gospel, a willingness to defend your own integrity, and an openness to implement confrontational techniques, under the guidance of the Spirit, may all be necessary ingredients for you properly to "shepherd the flock of God that he purchased with his own blood" (Acts 20:28—NASV).

Endnotes

1.   John Calvin, *Calvin's Commentaries: Vol. 21*. Translated by Wm. Pringle from the original Latin, dated Nov. 29, 1549, 22 vols. (Grand Rapids: Baker Book House, 1979) p. 298.

5
Confrontational Preaching and Pastoral Care

Introduction

Confrontational Preaching is essential for pastoral care. People fall into many traps of deceit. Confrontational Preaching calls for right responses to the choices and pressures of life.

Common Pastoral Care Issues

People make choices in the common areas of dating and marriage, finances, education, employment, entertainment, and recreation. These areas seem benign enough not to warrant confrontation. Yet, establishing the Lordship of Jesus Christ in these areas can take some doing.

Dating, Courtship, and Marriage

For example, Christians are forbidden to marry non-Christians (1 Cor. 7:39). You marry whom you date. Yet, many young men and women who claim to belong to Jesus are dating non-Christians. These things ought not to be. "What fellowship has light with darkness?" (cf. 2 Cor. 6:14; Eph. 5:11) If Christ is really alive in Suzie, she has nothing in common with Mr. "Party Animal" Doe, or even Mr. "He's-the-sweetest-guy-and-a-real-gentlemen-the-Christian-men-I-know-could-take-some-lessons-from-him" Sam Business Associate. To be a real Christian is to follow Christ. Suzie, if Joe "Swell Guy" is not following Christ, you and he are walking in opposite directions. It's time to wake up, girl. Repent of your lust and insecurity, and come back to your first love! (cf. Rev. 2:4,5) "And this I say for your own benefit; not to put a restraint upon you, but to promote what is seemly, and to secure undistracted devotion to the Lord" (1 Cor. 7:35—NASV).

Let me cut a bit deeper with this application. If you are a Christian, following God with all your heart—perhaps with the hope of entering full time Christian service some day—you have no business dating a nominal Christian. "Discipleship dating" is about as effective as "evangelistic dating"; that is, not at all. As one who has been in ministry for over 20 years, I have seen men compromise their calling because they desired a wife more than they valued God's call. The same can be said of some women. People need to be warned that dating can be a dangerous business. This may not be the kind of preaching you want to do, but if you are to be a good steward of the manifold wisdom of God, you must (cf. 1 Cor 7:25-35).

One goal of Confrontational preaching is to "secure undistracted devotion to the Lord" (1 Cor. 7:35). Undistracted devotion to the Lord will not come to the one who has failed to bring God's perspective into his or her dating experience.

Finances

Finances are another area in which your people make daily decisions. Jesus taught more on money than he did about heaven or hell. He must consider money matters to be important. When did you last preach a *series* of sermons on finances? When did you last preach a *single* sermon on finances? God's people are making and spending money. Where? On what? Jesus said, "Where your treasure is, there will your heart be also" (Lk. 12:34). Where are your people storing up their treasures?

Tithing is an important topic. Some fail to see it as a New Testament mandate. Jesus included tithing in the list of things to be retained (Matt. 23:23). He mentioned it in one of his most confrontational sermons.

> "Woe to you, scribes and Pharisees, hypocrites! For you tithe mint and dill and cumin, and have neglected the weightier provisions of the law: justice and mercy and faithfulness; but these are the things you should have done *without neglecting the others"* (Matt. 23:23—NASV, emphasis mine).

"The others" mentioned above refer to tithing. Jesus did not set tithing aside, he expanded it. "So therefore, no one of you can be My disciple who does not give up all his own possessions" (Lk. 14:33—NASV). If you possess the things you own, you are a mammon-possessed man, and no mammon-possessed man is going to be a good steward of another man's property. "The earth is the Lord's and the fullness thereof; the world, and they that dwell therein" (Psalm 14:1—KJV). Not only does the tithe belong to God, but all that a person possesses—including himself—belongs to God. And God wants it all!

The work of God has for years suffered at the hands of greedy men, who have refused to give God a tithe and yield full rights of ownership to God. If every Christian was a good steward of God's resources, world missions would never lack for finance. If every Christian was a good steward of God's wealth, no local church would have to use gimmicks, or even "stewardship drives" to refurbish or build adequate facilities.

Haggai preached this same sermon in 520 B.C. to a remnant who had returned to the promised land from Babylonian captivity. Kenneth Taylor's paraphrase records the sermon as follows:

> 2 "Why is everyone saying it is not the right time for rebuilding my Temple?" asks the Lord.
> 3,4 His reply to them is this: "Is it then the right time for you to live in luxurious homes, when the Temple lies in ruins? 5 Look at the result: 6 You plant much but harvest little. You have scarcely enough to eat or drink, and not enough clothes to keep you warm. Your income disappears, as though you were putting it into pockets filled with holes!
> 7 "Think it over," says the Lord of Hosts. "Consider how you have acted, and what has happened as a result! . . .
> 9 "You hope for much but get so little. And when you bring it home, I blow it away—it doesn't last at all. Why? Because my Temple lies in ruins and you don't care. Your only concern is your own fine homes" (Haggai 1:2-7,9—The Living Bible, Paraphrased).

What are your people doing with God's money? It's time for you to help them decide where God's money should go. I am not suggesting that you use hard sell techniques when you take the offering. I am saying, "Preach the word": God's Word includes priorities for financial management.

The issues mentioned at the beginning of this chapter—dating and marriage, finances, education, employment, entertainment, and recreation—at times demand confrontational preaching for proper pastoral care. There are other issues that demand even stronger confrontation.

Unusual, But Real, Pastoral Care Issues

When Paul left Ephesus he charged the pastors,[1] saying, "Be on guard for yourselves and for all the flock . . ." (Acts 20:28).

The word for "guard" is *prosechete*. (It is used also in Lk. 17:3, 21:34; Acts 5:35.) It means, to

> pay close attention to, hold on to, give oneself to (used of being addicted to wine, or being fond of wine, 1 Tim. 3:8); be on guard, watch, be careful . . . [2]

It's basic meaning is to watch closely; therefore, to guard. The main items the preacher guards against are false doctrines and false teachers. As Paul reveals in Acts 20:29-31,

> 29 I know that after my departure savage wolves will come in among you, not sparing the flock;
> 30 and from among your own selves men will arise, speaking perverse things, to draw away the disciples after them.
> 31 Therefore be on the alert . . .

The Cults

Pastoring in the San Francisco Bay Area has given me a great deal of exposure to the cults and to the occult. However, living in non-metropolitan areas does not exempt you from dealing with "Christian" doctrinal aberrations, such as Mormonism, Jehovah's Witnesses, and the Moonies. Nor does it inoculate you from witchcraft or the occult. There are terrible things afoot in the world today, and you must confront them boldly.

In the early 80's a teen-age girl was "abducted" from our church by a cult that was colloquially referred to as "The

Blanket People." They wore (dingy) white clothing and carried bed rolls on their backs. They had interesting dietary "requirements" that included marijuana. The girl in our church had just been converted to Christ from a non-Christian background and she had no discernment. This group talked about love, peace, and Jesus (they claimed Jesus had returned to earth, and was living somewhere in the Mohave Desert—cf. Matt. 24:4-5). They claimed to offer her a simpler lifestyle, with what seemed to her to be the same faith that she had just received. Therefore, she joined their group and left town with them. We began to pray fervently for her return.

She did return, but to the emergency room of a local hospital. She had lost touch with reality. Either the police found her, or she realized she needed psychiatric help. We heard of her whereabouts, and began praying for her healing and release from the hospital.

When she returned to the Bible study held in my home we welcomed her back enthusiastically. It would have been wonderful if that were the end of her struggle. In many ways it was just the beginning. She needed a full dose of Biblical truth to confront the lies she had been told while she was with the Blanket People. Your people also need a well balanced diet of Biblical truth if they are to be safe-guarded from "wolves in sheep's clothing" (Matt. 7:15).

Although this type of preaching is sometimes avoided by pastors, it is a necessary part of your pastoral duty. You may believe this kind of confrontation is better handled in a one-on-one counseling session. The fact is, not everyone who needs this type of safeguard will come to counseling to get it. The pulpit is the surest access you have into the minds and hearts of people who might be susceptible to occult or cultic overtures. Protect God's people by confronting the cults as you hold up God's standard of truth. Paul told Titus to "rebuke them sharply, that they might be sound in the faith" (Titus 1:13).

Paul demonstrated his willingness to practice what he preached when he "withstood (Peter) to his face, because he

(Peter) stood condemned" (Gal. 2:11). (This was a "cult" issue; i.e., Peter was siding with the Judaizers.)

God is no respecter of persons; the preacher cannot be either. The truth of the Gospel and the safety of the flock are what matter most.

The chief tool that the pastor has been given for guarding the flock is the Word of God (see 2 Tim. 4:1-5). Paul reiterates this fact in Acts 20:32.

> And now I commend you to God and to the word of His grace, which is able to build you up and to give you the inheritance among all those who are sanctified (NASV).

The Amplified Bible reads,

> And now, brethren, I commit you to God—that is, I deposit you in His charge, entrusting you to His protection and care. And I commend you to the Word of His grace—to the commands and counsels and promises of His unmerited favor. It is able to build you up and to give you [your rightful] inheritance among all God's set-apart ones—those consecrated, purified and transformed of soul.

The charge to "guard" goes hand-in-glove with the Word of God's grace. Apart from God's word there can be no true safety for the people of God, nor can there be any true standard for the preacher. To guard yourself and the flock, you must preach God's word confrontationally.

Other Areas of Deception, and Pastoral Care

Cults are not the only deception a pastor needs to protect God's people from. One reason that your proclamation must be confrontational is that there are so many types of deception in the world (cf. Rev. 12:9). The New Testament uses three different Greek words for deception and speaks of deception in areas of both thought and behavior.

The three Greek words used in the (King James) New Testament for "deceive" are, *"planao"*, *"apatao"*, and *"exapatao"*. We will look at these in turn.

Planao—Sheep in Danger of Straying Away

Jesus said, "See to it that no one misleads you. For many will come in my name, saying, 'I am the Christ,' and will mislead many" (Matt. 24:4,5—NASV). The Greek word translated *mislead* (*deceive* in the KJV) is "*planao*: to roam (from safety, truth, or virtue):—go astray, deceive, err, seduce, wander, be out of the way."[3] The people under your charge (cf. Acts 20:21) are at risk of roaming from safety if they do not have a steady diet of the Word of God that includes head-to-head confrontation with the false Christ's of this world. Jesus said that deceivers would be so numerous and plausible in the last days, that, if it were possible, "they shall deceive the very elect" (Matt. 24:24). In addition to the private ministry of the Spirit,[4] believers need protective preaching. Ephesians 4:14 says that crafty men "lie in wait to deceive" (*planao*).

Some fall into the deception that they can live like devils and still call themselves Christians. John, using the word *planao*, confronts this false concept head on.

> 7 Little children, let no one deceive you; the one who practices righteousness is righteous, just as He is righteous;
>
> 8 and the one who practices sin is of the devil; for the devil has sinned from the beginning. The Son of God appeared for this purpose, that He might destroy the works of the devil.

Another type of deception that falls under the rubric of *planao* is self-deception. 1 John 1:8 reads, "If we say that we have no sin, we deceive (*planao*) ourselves, and the truth is not in us."

A lady in a church I pastored in San Francisco believed in sinless perfection. She believed that a Christian could come into a state of perfection in this life. If you believe perfection is possible in this life, then you must attain it. To do less would be to disobey God. This lady thought that she had attained perfection. The result was that she would never ask forgiveness for anything. Why? Because she refused to believe that she ever did anything wrong.

Perhaps you've heard the story about the preacher who asked his congregation, "Has anyone ever heard of somebody, other than Jesus Christ, who was perfect?" A man in the back row stood to his feet, raised his hand and said, "Yes pastor, my wife's first husband."

The truth is, nobody is perfect. That is not to be used as an excuse for the Christian to sin (cf. 1 Jn. 2:1). It is to be understood as an ongoing battle against sin (see 1 John 1:8; Gal. 5:17, and James 1:14). The sin principle is not eradicated from the Christian's life at conversion: "If we say that we have no sin, we are deceiving ourselves, and the truth is not in us" (1 Jn. 1:8). Therefore, you cannot claim to be sinlessly perfect and be living consistently with the biblical revelation. The epistle of First John reveals that a sin principle continues in the life of the believer (1:8), that confession is the way to forgiveness (1:9), and that denying individual acts of sin insults God (1:10). Because forgiveness is linked to confession, it is imperative for you to admit your sin.

"He who conceals his transgressions will not prosper, but he who confesses and forsakes them will find compassion" (Prov. 28:13). Self-deception is a dangerous trap because it will cause a person to deny his sin even when he is knee deep in it. If not recognized and repented of in time, the quicksand of self-deception will swallow him alive. Confront self-deception as you would any other ravenous wolf.

Apatao—Sheep in Danger from Deceptive Desires

Apatao is another Greek word translated "deceive." It means, "deceive, cheat, mislead."[5] It was also used of sexual seduction.[6] The context of this word in the New Testament is improper behavior. That is, don't let others deceive you into thinking you can live immorally and still go to heaven (cf., Eph. 5:6), and do not deceive yourself into thinking that you don't need to control your tongue, for example (cf., James 1:26).

5 For this you know with certainty, that no immoral or impure person or covetous man, who is an idolater, has an inheritance in the kingdom of Christ and God.

6 Let no one deceive you with empty words, for because of these things the wrath of God comes upon the sons of disobedience (Eph. 5:5,6—NASV).

And,

If anyone thinks himself to be religious, and yet does not bridle his tongue but deceives his own heart, this man's religion is worthless (Jas. 1:26).

The noun form of this word means "deception, & deceitfulness."[7] In the New Testament, it refers to *the seduction which comes from wealth* (Mt. 13:22; Mk. 4:19) in particular, and *the deceitfulness of sin*[8] (Hb. 3:13) in general. Eph. 4:22 says,

in reference to your former manner of life, you lay aside the old self, which is being corrupted in accordance with the lusts of deceit (NASV).

Arndt and Gingrich translates "the lusts of deceit" as "deceptive desire".[9] Christians bring into their lives deceptive desires; you must confront those desires.

Exapatao—Sheep in Danger of Being Wholly Seduced

The last New Testament word for "deceive", *exapatao*, is a compound form of the one just studied. It is compounded with the Greek preposition *ek*, meaning "out of." Therefore, it is to deceive someone out of something, or take someone out of something by the use of deception. Strong's definition is "*to seduce wholly*—beguile, deceive."[10] This word is used "of the serpent's deception of Eve in 2Cor. 11:3; & 1Tim. 2:14.—in the former passage it meant 'lead astray.'"[11] It is used of self-deception in 1Cor. 3:18. And it is used in connection with factious people. This connection with factious people carries the sense of the compounding of the word, because factious people (heretics) seduce people out of the safety and fellowship of the saints.

17 Now I urge you, brethren, keep your eye on those who cause dissensions and hindrances contrary to the teaching which you learned, and turn away from them.

18 For such men are slaves, not of our Lord Christ but of their own appetites; and by their smooth and flattering speech

they deceive the hearts of the unsuspecting
(Rom. 16:17-18,NASV).

Second Thessalonians uses *exapatao* to allude to those who bring a twisted theological position to the discussion of our eschatological hope (2 Thes. 2:3). Entire groups have been *wholly seduced* into thinking that Jesus was to come at a certain date. Not long ago a book was written with a title similar to, *88 Reasons why Jesus Christ is Returning in '88.* Although many sincere Christians bought into this doctrine, Jesus did not return in 1988. Those who warned their congregations not to buy into something so foolish can feel secure in knowing that they fulfilled their pastoral duty in that instance. Those who fell into the error need to be on the alert not to be wholly seduced next time. Keep alert! There are many pastoral care issues that need to be dealt with confrontationally.

Conclusion

The pulpit is one place where pastoral care must take place. When you face immorality in your church, you must sound an alarm. When you face inaccurate doctrine, you must sound an alarm. When you find factious people seducing sheep into error, or when you find people living in self-deception, you must come with confrontation. These are pastoral care issues. These can be dealt with from the pulpit.

I did not shrink from declaring to you anything that was profitable, and teaching you publicly and from house to house. Therefore be on the alert, remembering that night and day for a period of three years I did not cease to admonish each one with tears (Acts 20:30, 31—NASV).

That is confrontational preaching as pastoral care.

Endnotes

1. "The terms 'Bishop' and 'elder' were used interchangeably here as well as elsewhere in the New Testament (cf. Titus 1:5,7). In verse 28 'to feed' is literally 'to shepherd.' It is interesting to note that, though he had just spoken of 'the flock,' here he urged them to 'shepherd *the church.*' The three titles, then, (elder, bishop, and pastor) were used interchangeably for the same men." Frank Stagg, *The Book of Acts: The Early Struggle for an Unhindered Gospel* (Nashville: Broadman Press, 1955), p. 217

2. Barclay M. Newman, *A Concise Greek-English Dictionary of the N.T.* (London: United Bible Societies, 1971) p. 153

3. Spiros Zodhiates, *The Greek-Hebrew Rey Study Bible,* (Iowa Falls, Iowa: World Bible Publishers, Inc., 1984, 5th printing, 1988) *Greek Dictionary of the New Testament,* #4105, p. 58.

4. See 2 Tim. 1:14; Eph. 1:13; John 14:16,17; John 16:13,14, and 1 John 3:26-27 for a sampling of the guarding and teaching ministry of the Holy Spirit in the believer's life.

5. William F. Arndt, and F. Wilbur Gingrich, A *GREEK-ENGLISH LEXICON OF THE NEW TESTAMENT and Other Early Christian Literature* (Chicago: The University of Chicago Press, 1957) p. 81

6. Ibid.

7. Ibid.

8. Ibid.

9. Ibid.

10. Zodhiates, *op. cit.,* #1818, p. 29

11. William F. Arndt and F. Wilbur Gingrich, A *GREEK-ENGLISH LEXICON of The NEW TESTAMENT, and Other Early Christian Literature.* (Chicago: The University of Chicago Press, 1957, Twelfth Impression 1969) p. 272

6
Historical Examples
of Confrontational Preaching

Confrontational preaching is mandated both by the example of the New Testament preachers and the teaching of the New Testament writers. If you see the biblical necessity for Confrontational Preaching here are some examples from church history to encourage you along the way.

The early church retained many of the Apostolic confrontational preaching methods found in the New Testament. The use of the second person, sarcasm, commands, warnings, threatenings, and other forms of reproof, rebuke and exhortation appear frequently in early Christian sermons. For a season, however, the pulpit lost its power and sway with the people. This was true from A.D. 430 to A.D. 1112. In A.D. 430 Augustine died; in 1112 Bernard of Clairvaux entered the ministry. Both of these men had powerful pulpit ministries. The intervening years boasted none, as noted by Drs. Fant and Pinson.

> With the death of Chrysostom and of Augustine, a long dark night came upon preaching: the golden age of preaching in the early church came to an end . . . Not until the twelfth century does the darkness begin to lift. With the coming of men such as Bernard of Clairvaux the pace of preaching began to quicken: but prior to Bernard there stretches a span of seven hundred years of preaching void.[1]

The reason for this lack of power may be that sermons, during this "dark" period, had lost their confrontive edge and, therefore, their ability to persuade. In contrast to this period of powerless preaching are the sermons preached before A.D. 430 and following A.D. 1112. Many sermons preached before and after this so called "Dark Age of Preaching" contain confrontational methods. The following sermon excerpts demonstrate how confrontational techniques have been employed throughout church history.

Origen

Origen (Origenes Admantius, A.D. 185-254) preached a sort of running exegesis with much allegory. His sermons are more explanation than exhortation, thus less confrontational by nature. Yet even in his allegorized introduction to a sermon on the Song of Songs, he frequently uses the second person to address his audience.

> **You** must come out of Egypt and, when the land of Egypt lies behind **you**, **you** must cross the Red Sea if **you** are to sing the first song, saying: "Let us sing to the Lord, for He is gloriously magnified." But though **you** have uttered this first song, **you** are still a long way from the Song of Songs. Pursue **your** spiritual journey through the wilderness, until **you** come to "the well which the kings dug," so that there **you** may sing the second song. After that, come to the threshold of the holy land, that standing on the bank of Jordan **you** may sing the song of Moses" (emphasis mine).[2]

Origen used the second person and commands to keep the flow of his introduction moving and the demand on his listeners obvious. Regrettably, he abandons this practice two paragraphs later. The result is a significant diminution of applicability. His introduction is much more compelling than the body due, in part, to the presence of the second person and frequent commands.

Chrysostom

Chrysostom (John of Antioch, A.D. 347-407) was much more confrontational than Origen. Chrysostom lived about 150 years after Origen and "was a man of great courage"[3] who "attacked every significant social and spiritual evil of his day. No sin escaped his blistering condemnation."[4] Chrysostom was a confrontational preacher. Drs. Fant and Pinson call this confrontational element "relevance." Confrontational preaching is that! Chrysostom "dealt with current issues. He spoke to lawlessness, to injustice and oppression, to frivolous living, to sexual immorality, to prejudice, and especially to personal vice."[5] This is the point at which it's been said of preachers, "Now he's quit preachin', and gone to meddlin'." Fant and Pinson continue, "Because of his relevance, he lost his position and ultimately his life. Yet because he was relevant, he was a great preacher."[6] Confrontation increased Chrysostom's relevance.

Chrysostom used the second person, sarcasm, and categorization to rebuke a congregation that was dwindling due to amusements at "the hippodrome." This type of sermon might be fitting on a Sunday morning during football season.

> 1. AGAIN THERE ARE CHARIOT RACES and satanic spectacles in the hippodrome, and our congregation is shrinking. It is on this account and because I feared and anticipated the negligence which comes from ease and security that I exhorted you and encouraged you in your love not to squander the wealth you had won by fasting, nor to inflict on yourselves the outrage which comes from Satan's spectacles. As it seems, no profit came to you from this exhortation. See how some who heard my previous instruction have today rushed away. They gave up the chance to hear this spiritual discourse and have run off to the hippodrome.[7]

Following this section Chrysostom adds personal testimony. The Apostle Paul used personal testimony extensively when his authority or his Gospel were being challenged. Here Chrysostom uses it when he sees spiritual lethargy in his congregation.

> 2. With what zeal, tell me, shall I hereafter undertake my usual instruction, when I see that they no longer derive profit from my words, but that, the longer my discourses continue, the more, I might say, does their negligence increase? This makes my grief greater and their condemnation more grave. Not only is my grief increased, but so too has my discouragement. When a farmer sees that, after all his work and troubles, the earth produces no return for his labors but is no more productive than a stone, he is more hesitant thereafter to work the land, because he sees that his work is idle and in vain.[8]

Chrysostom does not stop with these methods of reproof alone. He commands his listeners to rebuke their wayward brethren for their backsliding and exhort them to return to church at the next service. Notice also the frequent use of "you" in the following example.

> 17. But what profit is there in such accusations when the guilty are not present to hear what is said? Even so, my exhortation will not be without purpose; for it is possible for them to get exact knowledge of all I have said through their association with you, and on the one hand to flee the devil's snare, and on the other to return to their spiritual nourishment. . . .

> 18. For when you leave here and take up the task of your brother's salvation, not only accusing and reproving him, but also counseling and encouraging him, showing the harm that comes from worldly amusement and the profit and benefit to be derived from our instruction, you have done all for the glory of God. And you have doubled your reward, both because you are producing great profit for your own salvation and because you have been eager to cure one of your own members. This is the glory of the Church, this is the commandment of our Saviour, namely, to look not only to one's own good but also to that of one's neighbor.[9]

Augustine

Augustine (A.D. 354-430) made very effective use of the second person as well as the imperative. The first example, given below, is from a sermon on the Lord's prayer; the second is from a Christmas sermon. In the first example, Augustine is commenting on the responsibility of the one who prays, "Forgive us our trespasses, as we forgive those who trespass against us."

> And so you ought to do; if not, you will perish. When your enemy asks pardon, forgive him at once. Is this too much for you? It would be much for you to love your enemy when he is cruel to you, but is it much to love a man who is beseeching you? You protest? You say he used to treat you unkindly, therefore you hate him now. Would that you had not hated him even then; would that when you were suffering

from his cruelty you had kept in mind the words of our Lord, "Father, forgive them, for they know not what they do!" This is what I should have much preferred, that even at the time when your enemy was angry with you, you had reflected on the Lord your God speaking in this manner. Perhaps you will counter, He did so; but He did it as the Lord, as the Christ, as the Son of God, as the sole-begotten One, as the Word made flesh. But what can I, a weak and sinful man, do? Well, if your Lord's example is too lofty for you, then consider the example of one of your fellowmen. St. Stephen was being stoned, and as they stoned him, he prayed on bended knees for his enemies: "Lord, lay not this sin to their charge." They were casting stones, not begging for forgiveness, and yet he prayed for them. I wish you were like him. Exert yourself! Why do you always drag your heart along the earth? Listen to me—lift up your heart, exert yourself, love your enemies![10]

What a powerful use of the second person and the imperative!

This second example from Augustine is for the preacher who is not yet convinced that you can use the second person without becoming purely visceral or pedestrian. Augustine addresses his audience using the second person throughout the following paragraph from his Christmas sermon. His use of the second person in no way compromises the wonder of the Incarnation, but rather it heightens the theological contrast between the depravity of man and the holiness of this Infant Saviour God, the Lord Jesus Christ.

See, O man, what God has become for you. Take to heart the lesson of this great humility, though the Teacher of it is still without speech. Once, in Paradise, you were so eloquent that you gave a name to every living being; but your Creator, because of you, lay speechless, and did not call even his mother by her name. You, finding yourself in a boundless estate of fruitful groves, destroyed yourself by having no regard for obedience; He, obedient, came as a mortal man to a poor, tiny lodging that by dying He might seek the return of him who had died. You, though you were only man, wished to be God; and you were lost. He, though He was God, wished to be man that He might find what had been lost. Human

85

pride pressed you down so that divine humility alone could lift you up.[11]

Bernard

Upon the death of Chrysostom (A.D. 407) and Augustine (A.D. 430) there came what has been called the Dark Ages of Preaching. This darkness was pierced by Bernard of Clairvaux (A.D. 1090-1153), who was Canonized by Alexander III in 1174, and made Doctor of the Church by Pius VIII, in 1830.

The following background information demonstrates the breadth of Bernard's pastoral concern, as expressed through his preaching.

> He had courage: he was not afraid to rebuke kings, to debate brilliant intellectuals, or to condemn the faults of his own church. He had compassion: he pleaded for mercy to be extended to the persecuted Jews and for concern to be demonstrated for the poor. He was involved in the issues of his day: he spoke about wealth and the use of money, government and civil power, prejudice, and purity of life.[12]

Bernard's preaching had a confrontational element that grew out of his deep piety. His preaching kept its focus on the heart of men and their need for genuine heart-felt repentance. That type of probing always has a confrontive element to it, even if it lacks specific confrontational categories. That is, it's easier to feel the confrontation in Bernard's words than to identify the specific confrontational technique. Perhaps the chief category, or technique, used by Bernard would be "contrast," much like John's contrasts between "light and dark" (John 1:4,5; 1 Jn. 1:5), "truth and lies" (1 Jn. 1:8; 2:21-22), "love and hate" (1 Jn. 4:20). Bernard uses contrast to confront the conscience of his congregation and bring them to repentance. He frequently refers to the contrast between "pride and humility." He also exposes the difference between merely outward (false) conversion, and inward (true) conversion. The following are a few examples of Bernard's probing words. First, a word on pride.

If the path appointed to lead us unto God were the path of loftiness, and if that were the way by which is shown the salvation of the Lord (Ps. 49:23), Oh, what would not men do in order to exalt themselves! How pitilessly they would overthrow and trample upon each other! How shamelessly they would stoop to the meanest practices and endeavour with might and main to mount aloft, so as to be placed over the heads of other men! . . . On the other hand, nothing is so easy as to humble oneself—all that is necessary is the desire. Dearest brethren, these are truths which render our pride absolutely inexcusable, and leave it without any veil, even the thinnest, under which to shelter.[13]

This second example contrasts an external conversion with a true spiritual conversion.

An external turning to God, unaccompanied by a conversion of the heart and spirit is nothing worth [i.e., "worth nothing"]. It is only a formal, not a true conversion, "having the appearance indeed of godliness but lacking the power thereof" (2 Tim. 3:5). Unhappy the man who, devoting all his attention to outward observances, remains ignorant of his interior, for "thinking himself to be something, whereas he is nothing, he deceiveth himself" (Gal. 6:3). . . .

My brother, consider carefully what is the object of thy love and of thy fear, what is the source of thy joy and of thy sadness, and thou shalt find a worldly spirit under the habit of religion, and under the tattered covering of an exterior conversion a perverted heart.[14]

This final example is between the evils of this present life on earth (especially those days spent in sinful acts or thoughts), and the future joys of heaven.

. . . the newness of this heavenly life will have little charm for him who has not yet begun to lament the evils of his old life, to lament the sins he has been guilty of, to lament the loss of time. If thou mournest not, it is manifest that thou art insensible to the wounds of thy soul and to the damage done to thy conscience. On the other hand, thou dost not desire the bliss in store as ardently as thou oughtest unless thou askest for it daily with sighs and tears: it is a sign that

that bliss is not sufficiently known to thee if it be not the case that thy soul "refuseth to be comforted" (Ps. 76:3) until it has been bestowed.[15]

Wyclif

Two hundred years following the renaissance of preaching under Bernard of Clairvaux, John Wyclif (A.D. 1324-84) sharpened his sword on his audiences. In addition to methods of confrontation already illustrated, Wyclif provides examples of sarcasm. Sarcasm has been used throughout the church age to drive home points. Wyclif, a pre-reformer, when pointing out the error of assuming Christ's body is literally in the Eucharist, used much sarcasm.

> For ye say that in every host each piece is the whole manhood of Christ, or full substance of Him. For ye say as a man may take a glass, and break the glass into many pieces, and His body is not parted. And this is a full subtle question to beguile an innocent fool, but will ye take heed of this subtle question, how a man may take a glass and behold the very likeness of his own face, and yet it is not his face, but the likeness of his face; for if it were his very face, then he must needs have two faces . . .[16]

Modern preaching looks quite tame in comparison to such preaching.

Savonarola

Gerolamo Savonarola (A.D. 1452-1498), referring to a vision he questioned if he should preach, said that after an all night vigil of prayer he heard these words:

> "Fool, dost thou not see that it is God's will that thou shouldst continue in the same path?" Wherefore I preached that day a terrible sermon. The sermon Savonarola referred to as "terrible" was a violent denunciation of the clergy and a condemnation of the habits of the people of Florence.[17]

An example of such a denunciation is one given against the clergy. In it he pulls the cloak off the sins of the clergy, leaving them exposed. This is an important aspect of confrontational preaching; it exposes and reproves evil. "And have no fellowship with the unfruitful works of darkness, but rather reprove them" (Eph. 5:11—KJV). The following is an example of Savonarola's reproof against a decadent clergy.

> They speak against pride and ambition, yet are plunged in both up to the eyes; they preach chastity, and maintain concubines; they prescribe fasting, and feast splendidly themselves.

Luther

How did the reformers refer to their audiences? Martin Luther (A.D. 1483-1546) labeled people and called names. For example, in a sermon on the need for sobriety and moderation in all things, Luther said, "Do not make a pig of yourself; remain a human." Two paragraphs later Luther states, "If you have been a pig, then stop being one." To name calling, Luther adds a command to stop a behavior. He then turns to illustration and reproof by quoting from an earlier well-known preacher: "Augustine said: I have known many who were drunkards and then ceased being drunkards. But you are today just as you were yesterday and you go on thinking that it is not sin."[20] Luther uses sarcasm as well: "Christmas and Pentecost mean nothing but beer. Christians should not walk around so bedizened that one hardly knows whether one is looking at a man or a beast. We Christians ought to be examples."[21]

Wesley

John Wesley (A.D. 1703-91) frequently used commands. In a sermon entitled, "On Worldly Folly," Wesley's comments on Jesus's parable of the rich man who doesn't know what to do with all his wealth becomes an opportunity for Wesley to command his listeners to

> disperse abroad, and give to the poor. Feed the hungry. Clothe the naked. Be a father to the fatherless, and a husband to the widow. Freely thou hast received; freely give.[22]

Do you give clear commands to your congregation as to how they can carry out the will of God? Don't leave it to guesswork. Give commands.

Wesley sought to make his commands crystal clear by using leading questions, "What shalt thou do? Why, are not those at the door whom God hath appointed to receive what thou canst spare?"[23]

Questions can also be used to confront the conscience. Paul used them: "Who has bewitched you?" (Gal. 3:1), and "Are you so foolish?" (Gal. 3:3) Wesley, in the sermon quoted above, returned to his theme three paragraphs later with a series of questions designed to convict and arouse the conscience.

> Canst thou find none that need the necessaries of life, that are pinched with cold or hunger; none that have not raiment to put on, or a place where to lay their head; none that are wasted with pining sickness; none that are languishing in prison? If you duly considered our Lord's words, "The poor have you always with you," you would no more ask, "What shall I do?"[24]

Whitefield

George Whitefield (A.D. 1714-70), a friend and classmate of John and Charles Wesley, and the noted orator of the Oxford "Holy Club," used many confrontational techniques. In a sermon entitled, "Soul Prosperity," Whitefield used sarcasm to convince his hearers of their need for diligence and perseverance.

> We may frequently sit under the gospel, but if we do not take a great deal of care, however orthodox we are, we shall fall into practical Antinomianism, and be contented that we were converted twenty or thirty years ago, and learn, as some Antinomians, "to live by faith." Thank God, say some, we met God so many months ago, but are not at all solicitous whether they met with him any more.[25]

Edwards

Perhaps the most famous confrontational sermon in history—due to its straight-forward style and frightening theme—is, "Sinners in the Hands of an Angry God," by Jonathan Edwards (A.D. 1703-1758). His most notable confrontational technique is the use of the second person. Note how frightening this use makes his sermon, and how compelling!

You shall be tormented in the presence of the holy angels, and in the presence of the Lamb; and when you shall be in this state of suffering, the glorious inhabitants of heaven shall go forth and look on the awful spectacle, that they may see what the wrath and fierceness of the Almighty is . . . but you must suffer it to all eternity. There will be no end to this exquisite horrible misery. When you look forward, you shall see a long for ever, a boundless duration before you, which will swallow up your thoughts, and amaze your soul; and you will absolutely despair of ever having any deliverance, any end, any mitigation, any rest at all. You will know certainly that you must wear out long ages, millions of millions of ages, in wrestling and conflicting with this almighty merciless vengeance; and then when you have so done, when so many ages have actually been spent by you in this manner, you will know that all is but a point to what remains.[26]

Drs. Fant and Pinson, critiquing "Sinners in The Hands of An Angry God," note the impact of singling out certain groups within the congregation and of referring directly to the audience.

The sentences are direct: there is an ascending force about the sermon as Edwards meticulously and relentlessly turns from picture to picture, from description to description. Few sermons have excelled this one for direct application; in various places Edwards addresses the old men, the middle-aged, and the children in his congregation. He repeatedly says "you," "this congregation," and "today."[27]

Sunday

Billy Sunday was a classic example of a confrontational preacher. Billy preached from 1891 to 1935. He was a converted baseball player and ex-drinker who became a traveling evangelist. A very colorful preacher, he used every technique of confrontation mentioned in this book. He used sarcasm, labeling, name calling, the second person, questions, and even ridicule.

He (Mr. Sunday) made sin absurd . . . as well as wicked; and he made the sinner ashamed of himself. He recovered for the Church the use of a powerful weapon, the barb of ridicule.[28]

Ellis continues his biography of Sunday by affirming the thesis of this book, "There are more instruments of warfare in the gospel armory than the average preacher commonly uses. . . . Sunday endeavored to employ them all. His favorites seemed to be humor, satire and scorn."[29] Another biographer noted that Billy "stormed up and down the platform scolding, insulting, imploring and demanding. He had to change his sweat-soaked suit after each meeting."[30] His was a robust religion.

"If nine-tenths of you were as weak physically as you are spiritually, you couldn't walk."[31]

"There's not a preacher in this town who won't put up his dukes and fight for Christ if you'll only get behind him. They would be doing it now only some of you fossilated, antiquated, old hypocrites begin to snort, snarl, and whine when they go after some of your pet sins. But I don't owe you anything. I'll skin you spiritually before I get through." Not only did Sunday "skin" them, but he poured on salt, then loved them to Jesus.[32]

Billy Sunday was the most successful evangelist of his day. When the world population was only one and one-half billion, and America's population only 110 million, "over one million converts walked the sawdust trail, grasping the evangelist's hand as a symbol of accepting Jesus Christ as Saviour."[33] To accept Christ as Savior under Billy Sunday's ministry was not the "bless me believism" seen in much of America today. His message demanded repentance.

Like Chrysostom, Wesley, and Luther before him, Sunday knew how to tackle sins of the day. Drugs and immorality are paramount vices today; in his day it was alcohol. To "men-only" crowds, Sunday frequently preached against the evils of "grog shops" and "booze." Through Sunday's anti-booze sermons hundreds of saloons closed, thousands of drunkards were reformed, and numerous cities voted to become "dry." Some of the confrontational techniques he employed were sarcasm, labeling, name calling, personal testimony, and the second person. Billy used all of these techniques in a sermon he preached in the year of 1908, in Pittsburgh, Pennsylvania.

Billy used sarcasm to isolate and condemn the use of alcohol. "Whisky is all right in its place, but its place is in hell. And I want to see everyone put it there as soon as possible."[34]

Sunday was not content to stop with the vice; he used labeling and name calling to attack the institutions and the men who made a living off the selling of alcohol. His tirades were virulent and fearless.

> "The saloon is a liar. There are twelve thousand saloon-keepers in New York City and eight thousand of them have criminal records. I don't think Pittsburgh is too far behind."
>
> He stood at the pulpit for only a minute. His fists were balled up like a fighter entering the ring for hard-hitting, no-holds-barred boxing. Only a minute, and then he flew into action.
>
> "Yes, the saloon is a liar. Every plot that was ever hatched against the government and law was born and bred and crawled out of the grog shop to damn this country."[35]

To labeling and name calling Sunday added personal testimony.

> With a great leap Billy was on top of the pulpit, arms outstretched, pleading with the vast congregation to take their stand for God. . . . "I've had more sneers and scoffs and insults, and had my life threatened from one end of this land to the other by this God-forsaken gang of thugs and cutthroats, because I have come out uncompromisingly against them. I've taken more dirty, vile insults from this low-down bunch than from anyone on earth . . ."[36]

Billy did not want to stand alone in his fight against the evils of his day any more than he wanted to stand alone in his salvation. When he made his appeal he used the second person to enlist his audience to join him in the fight.

> For one hour and forty-five minutes he preached, shedding coat, collar, cuffs, and tie in the process. "The saloon feeds on our boys and destroys the young manhood of our country . . . Are you going to let these boys be destroyed or are you going to take your stand for God and country? Can you be counted on to protect your wives and homes, your

mothers and the children and the manhood of America? . . .
I've done it for your boys and your wives, and for you.
How about it, will you come and take my hand and say, 'Bill,
I'll take my stand against booze the very first chance I get.'"[37]

Thousands responded to Billy Sunday's appeals. Sunday, like many before him, had a burning desire to lead men to Christ, and he was unafraid to reprove the ills of his day. As a result, not only did he see one million people converted to Christ through his ministry, but he saw his society impacted by the Gospel of the Lord Jesus Christ.

Conclusion

The preachers who have gained a hearing and moved the course of nations have preached confrontationally. If you are only concerned with keeping your job, ignore this exhortation. But if you want demons to tremble and heaven to rejoice at your words, then preach truth confrontationally! John Knox, John Wesley, and the Apostle Paul all accepted riots as potential by-products of their preaching. Yet they saw results in their day! Time and space do not permit me to give examples of Finney, Moody, Knox, Bunyan, and a host of other preachers who illustrate that confrontational preaching did not end with the deaths of the Apostles and early martyrs.

When you are preaching under the unction of the Holy Spirit and you feel yourself ready to fire away, don't shut the fire up in your bones. Fire away!

There are over twenty centuries of precedents. Every great preacher has used techniques of confrontational preaching found in this book. Now it's your turn.

Endnotes

1. Clyde E. Fant, Jr. and William M. Pinson, Jr. *20 Centuries of Great Preaching: An Encyclopedia of Preaching* (Waco, Texas: WORD BOOKS, Publisher) Volume One: Biblical Sermons to Savonarola; A.D. 27-1498. pp. 57-58

2. Clyde E. Fant, Jr. and William M. Pinson, Jr. *20 Centuries of Great Preaching,* (Waco, Texas: Word Books, Publisher, 1971) Vol. I, p. 38, quoting Origen's "First Homily."

3. Clyde E. Fant, Jr. and William M. Pinson, Jr. *20 Centuries of Great Preaching: An Encyclopedia of Preaching* (Waco, Texas: WORD BOOKS, Publisher, 1971) VOLUME ONE, Biblical Sermons to Savonarola, A.D. 27-1498. p. 55

4. Ibid.

5. Ibid.

6. Ibid.

7. Ibid., p.63

8. Ibid.

9. Ibid., pp. 67-68

10. Fant and Pinson, *20 Centuries,* Vol. I, p. 134

11. Ibid., p. 138

12. Fant and Pinson, *20 Centuries,* Vol. 1, p. 145

13. Fant and Pinson, 20 *Centuries,* Vol. I, p. 154

14. Ibid., p. 154

15. Ibid., p. 155

16. Fant and Pinson, *20 Centuries,* vol. I, p. 253

17. Ibid., vol. I, p. 269

18. Ibid. Vol. I, p. 271

19. Fant and Pinson, *20 Centuries,* Vol. II, pp. 15,16

20. Ibid., p. 16

21. Ibid.

22. John Wesley, *The Works of John Wesley,* Vol. VII, (Peabody, Massachusetts: HENDRICKSON PUBLISHERS, INC., reprinted 1984, from the 1872 edition issued by Wesleyan Methodist Book Room, London), p. 306.

23. Ibid.

24. Ibid., p. 307

25. Fant and Pinson, 20 *Centuries,* Vol. III, p. 162

26. Ibid.

27. Fant and Pinson, 20 *Centuries,* Vol. III, p. 53

28. William T. Ellis, *"Billy" Sunday: The Man and His Message* (Chicago: Moody Press, 1959) pp. 76-77

29. Ibid.

30. Lee Thomas, *Billy Sunday* (Van Nuys, California: Bible Voice, 1975) p. 15

31. Ellis, p. 73

32. Thomas, pp. 16,17

33. Thomas, p. 14

34. Robert A. Allen, *Billy Sunday: Home Run to Heaven* (Milford, Michigan: Mott Media, 1985) pp. 92-94

35. Ibid.

36. Ibid.

37. Ibid.

Bibliography

Abbott-Smith, G. *A Manual Greek Lexicon of the New Testament* New York: Charles Scribner's Sons, 1936.

Adams, Jay E. "Antithesis vs. Continuum." A lecture given to D. Min. students at Westminster Theological Seminary in California, January, 1985.

Adams, Jay E. *Preaching to the Heart.* Phillipsburg, New Jersey: Presbyterian and Reformed Publishing Company, 1983.

Allen, Robert A. *Billy Sunday: Home Run to Heaven.* Milford, Michigan: Mott Media, 1985.

Analytic Greek Lexicon, The. Grand Rapids: Zondervan, 11th printing, 1975.

Arndt, William F., and Gingrich, F. Wilbur. *A Greek-English Lexicon of the New Testament and Other Early Christian Literature.* Chicago: The University of Chicago Press, 1957.

Bibles:
The Amplified Bible
The Berkeley Version (Modern Language)
The Greek New Testament
The Jerusalem Bible
The King James
The Living Bible
The New American Standard
The New International Version
The Revised Standard Version

Calvin, John. *Calvin's Commentaries*. Vol. 21. Translated by Wm. Pringle from the original Latin, dated November 29, 1549, 22 vols. Grand Rapids:Baker Book House, 1979.

Calvin, John. "A French Sermon used as a Footnote Comment, in The Epistle to Titus." John Calvin's Commentaries. 21:298-299. Translated by Rev. Wm. Pringle. Grand Rapids: Baker Book House, 1979.

Choisy, Eugene. "Beza, Theodore." In *The New Shaff-Herzog Encyclopedia of Religious Knowledge*, 10:78-81. Edited by Samual Macauley Jackson, and others. 15 vols. Grand Rapids: Baker Book House, reprinted 1977.

Chrysostom (John of Antioch). "The Sixth Instruction." In *20 Centuries of Great Preaching*. 1:63-69. Edited by Clyde Fant, Jr. and William Pinson, Jr. 13 vols. Waco, TX: Word Books, Publisher, 1971.

Cromey, The Rev. Robert, Rector. "Dignity for Homosexual People." Sermon text at Trinity Church, San Francisco, CA, March 10, 1985.

Culver, Robert D. "*Nabi*. Spokesman, prophet." In *Theological Wordbook of the Old Testament*. 2:544-545. Edited by R. Laird Harris, Gleason L. Archer, Jr., and Bruce K. Waltke. 2 vols. Chicago: Moody Press, 1980.

Daane, James. *Preaching with Confidence: A Theological Essay on the Power of the Pulpit*. Grand Rapids: Wm. B. Eerdmans Publishing Company, 1980.

Ellis, William T. *"Billy" Sunday: The Man and His Message* Chicago: Moody Press, 1959

Enslin, Morton S. "Preaching from the New Testament: An Open Letter to Preachers." In *The Joy of Study: Papers on New Testament and Related Subjects*, presented to honor FREDERICK CLIFTON GRANT, edited by Sherman E. Johnson. New York: Macmillan, 1951.

Fant, Clyde E., Jr., and Pinson, William M., Jr. "Biography of Chrysostom." In *20 Centuries of Great Preaching*, 1:53-62. 13 vols. Waco, Texas: Word Books, Publ., 1971.

Fant, Clyde E. Jr., and Pinson, William M.,Jr. "Biography of George Whitefield." In *20 Centuries of Great Preaching*, 3:107-116. 13 vols. Waco, Texas: Word Books Publ., 1971.

Fant, Clyde E. Jr., and Pinson, William M., Jr. "Biography of Girolamo Savonarola," In *20 Centuries of Great Preaching*, 1:261-272. 13 vols. Waco, Texas: Word Books, Publ., 1971.

Friedrich, Gerhard. *Theological Dictionary of the New Testament*, 3:683-718. Edited by Gerhard Friedrich and Gerhard Kittel. 10 vols. Grand Rapids: Eerdmans, 1964-1976.

Haddal, Ingvar. *John Wesley: A Biography*. New York and Nashville: Abingdon Press, 1961.

Hendricks, William. "Jeremiah in Monologue" A video-tape presentation on file at Golden Gate Baptist Theological Seminary Library, Mill Valley, CA.

Jackson, Samuel Macauley. "Calvin, John." In *The New Shaff-Herzog Encyclopedia of Religious Knowledge*, 2:353-359. Edited by Samual Macauley Jackson, and others. 15 vols. Grand Rapids: Baker Book House, reprinted 1977.

Jefferson, Charles Edward. *The Minister as Prophet*. Grand Rapids: Zondervan, 1905. The George Shepard *Lectures on Preaching* at Bangor Theological Seminary, 1904-05.

Lachenmann, Eugene. "Servetus, Michael (Miguel Serveto)." In *The New Schaff-Herzog Encyclopedia of Religious Knowledge*, 10:371-373. Edited by Samuel Macauley Jackson, and George William Gilmore. 15 vols. Grand Rapids: Baker Book House, reprinted 1977.

Lindsell, Harold. "Battle for The Bible" Seminar, at *Congress on the Bible,* San Diego, CA, 1983.

Lloyd-Jones, D. Martyn. *Preaching & Preachers*. Grand Rapids: Zondervan Publ. House, July, 1971.

Luther, Martin. "Sermon on Soberness and Moderation." In *20 Centuries of Great Preaching*. 2:12-18. Edited by Clyde Fant, Jr. and William Pinson, Jr. Waco, TX: Word Books, Publisher, 1971.

Murillo, Mario. *No More War Games*. Chatsworth, CA: Anthony Douglas Publishing Co., 1987.

Newman, Barclay M. *A Concise Greek-English Dictionary of the N.T.* London: United Bible Societies, 1971.

Origen, "The First Homily." In *20 Centuries of Great Preaching* 1:38-49. Edited by Clyde Fant, and Wm. Pinson, 13 vols. 1971.

Rienecker, Fritz. *A Linguistic Key To The Greek New Testament*. 2 vols. Translated and revised by Cleon L. Rogers, Jr. Grand Rapids: Zondervan, 1980.

Robertson, A. T. *A Grammar of the Greek New Testament in The Light of Historical Research.* Nashville, Tennessee: Broadman Press, 1934.

Robertson, A. T. *Word Pictures in the New Testament.* Vol. IV. 6 vols. Nashville, Tennessee: Broadman Press, 1931.

Sproul, R. C. "What's Going On Here?" in *Table Talk*, issue entitled "The Power of Preaching." Walk Thru the Bible Ministries, Inc. under license granted by Ligonier Ministries, Inc., March 1989.

Spurgeon, Charles Haddon. "Sermons Likely to Win Souls." In *The Soul Winner.* Grand Rapids: Eerdmans, reprinted 1963.

Spurgeon, Charles Haddon. "The Overflowing Cup," in *The Metropolitan Tabernacle Pulpit*, Vol. XXI, 1875. Pasadena, Texas: Pilgrim Publications, 1971.

Stagg, Frank. *The Book of Acts: The Early Struggle for an Unhindered Gospel.* Nashville: Broadman Press, 1955.

Stalker, James, D.D. *The Preacher and His Models.* New York: Hooder and Stoughton; George H. Doran Company, 1891.

Stott, John R. W. *Between Two Worlds: The Art of Preaching in the Twentieth Century.* Grand Rapids: Wm. B. Eerdmans Publishing Company, 1981.

Swindoll, Charles. "Taking the Ho-Hum Out of Your Preaching" A seminar given at *Congress on Biblical Exposition*, Anaheim, CA, c. 1987.

Thielecke, Helmut. *Encounter with Spurgeon.* Philadelphia: Fortress Press, 1963.

Thomas, Lee. *BILLY SUNDAY*. Van Nuys, CA: Bible Voice, 1974

Tozer, A. W. "How the Lord Leads." In *The Alliance Weekly*. Nyack, New York: Christian Publications. January 2, 1957.

Vine, W. E. *The Expanded Vine's Expository Dictionary of New Testament Words*. Edited by John R. Kohlenberger III, with James A Swanson. Minneapolis, Minnesota: Bethany House Publishers, 1984.

Walter, Otis M. *Speaking to Inform and Persuade*. New York: The Macmillan Company, 1966; sixth printing, 1970.

Warfield, Benjamin B. "Calvinism." In *The New Shaff-Herzog Encyclopedia of Religious Knowledge*, 2:359-364. Edited by Samuel Macauley Jackson, and others. 15 vols. Grand Rapids: Baker Book House, reprinted 1977.

Webster's New Twentieth Century Dictionary of The English Language: Unabridged (second edition). United States: Wm. Collins+World Publishing Co., Inc. 1977.

Webster's New World Dictionary of the American Language: College Edition. Cleveland and New York: The World Publishing Company, 1959.

Wesley, John. "Sermon CXIX. On Worldly Folly." In *The Works of John Wesley*. 7:305-311. 14 vols. Peabody, MASS: Hendrickson Publishers, Inc. 1984.

White, Newport J. D. *The Expositor's Greek Testament*. Vol. IV. Edited by W. Robertson Nicoll. Grand Rapids: Eerdmans. 1970.

Whitefield, George. "Soul Prosperity." In *20 Centuries of Great Preaching.* 3:159-169. Edited by Clyde Fant,Jr. and William Pinson, Jr. 13 vols. Waco, TX: Word Books, Publisher, 1971.

Wigram, George V. *The Englishman's Greek Concordance of the New Testament,* Ninth Edition Grand Rapids: Zondervan, 1970.

Wilkinson, Bruce and Boa, Kenneth. *Talk Thru The Bible.* Nashville, Camden, New York: Thomas Nelson Publishers, 1983.

Wyclif, John. "Christ's Real Body Not in the Eucharist." In *20 Centuries of Great Preaching.* 1:2249-257. Edited by Clyde Fant, Jr. and William Pinson, Jr. 13 vols. Waco, TX: Word Books, Publisher, 1971.

Zodhiates, Spiros. *The Greek-Hebrew Key Study Bible.* Iowa Falls, Iowa: World Bible Publishers, Inc., 1984, 5th printing, 1988.